EyE
-OF THE BEHOLDER-

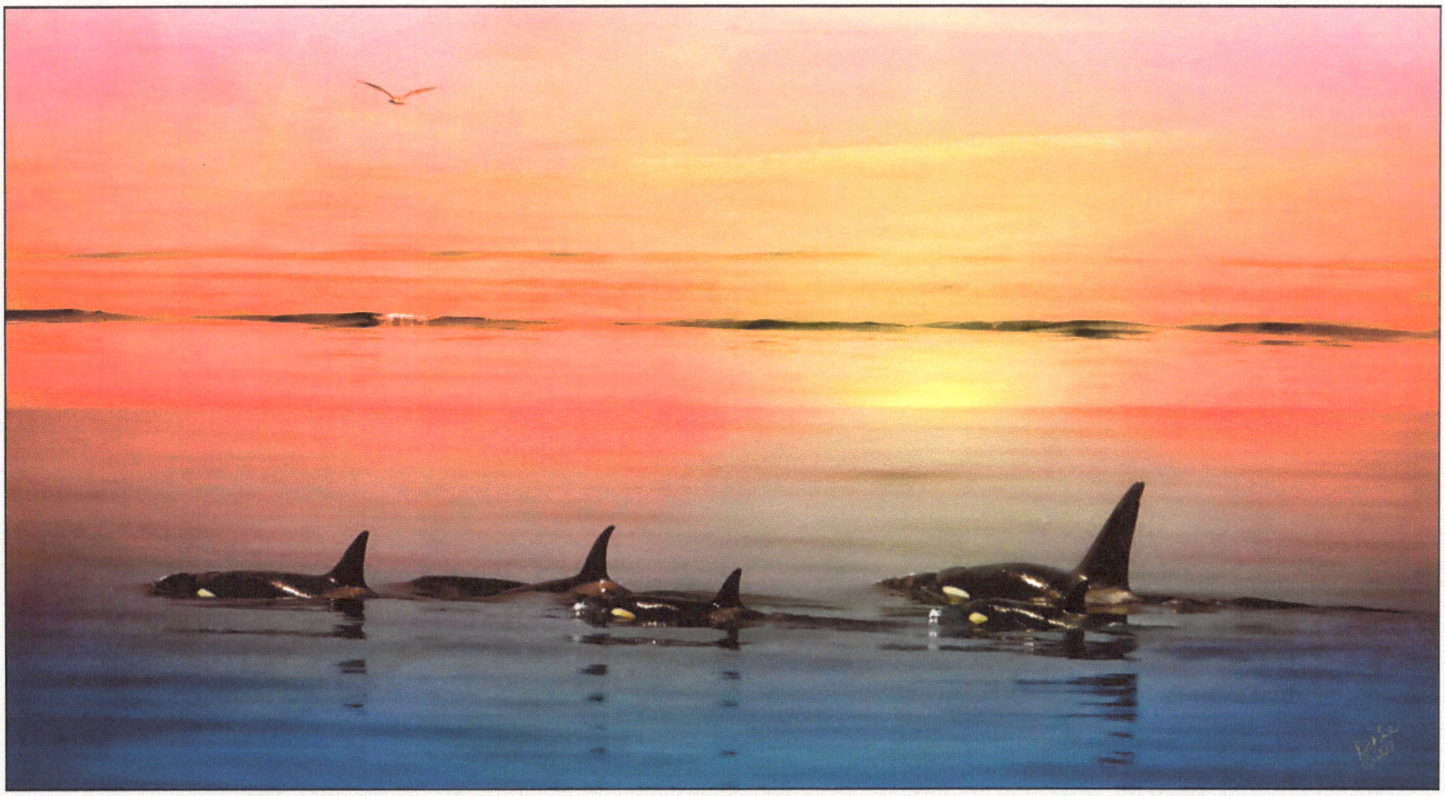

A collection of favorite photographs by Landscape and Wildlife photographer Rick Lawler

www.whidbeyphotos.com

EyE
-OF THE BEHOLDER-

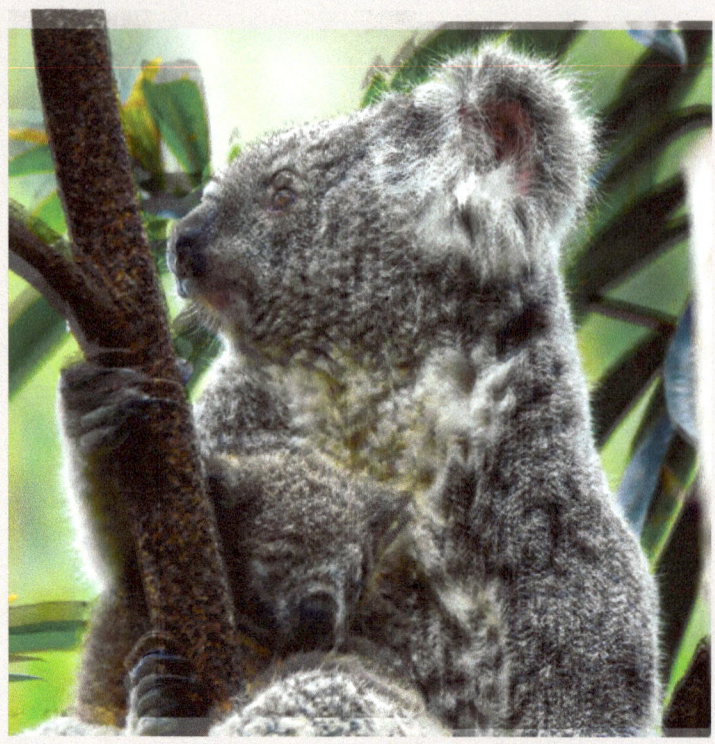

Copyright © 2020
by
Rick Lawler

All Rights Reserved

Printed in the U.S.A.
ISBN 978-1-930322-24-0

No part of this book may be reproduced or transmitted in any form or by any means, electronic, graphic, optical or mechanical, including photocopying, recording, taping, electronic data, internet packets, or by any other information storage or retrieval method without written permission of the publisher. For information contact MinRef Press, 3930 Affinity Lane #116, Bellingham, WA 98226.

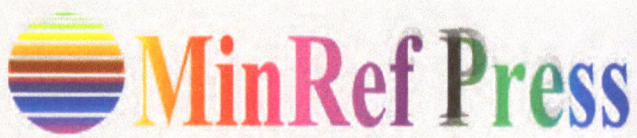 MinRef Press

Contact the Author at:
3930 Affinity Lane #116
Bellingham, WA 98226
minref@gmail.com * www.minref.com

www.whidbeyphotos.com

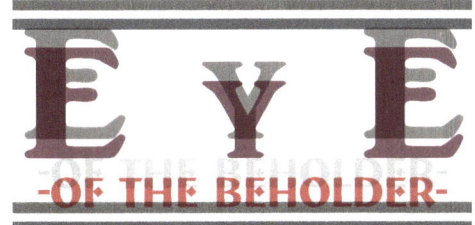

EYE
-OF THE BEHOLDER-

This volume is a collection of some of the favorite photographs I've taken over the past several years. There is no rhyme nor reason to the selections; they are simply favorites. They were taken close to home and half-way around the world. Some have been converted to digital art. Others have been adjusted, cropped, and designed.

You can see more of my images at my online gallery www.whidbeyphotos.com. You can even purchase a print there, if you so desire. Or just enjoy looking around. New photos are added from time-to-time as I finish processing them.

I've been a photographer since high school. I was a photographer for my high school yearbook and later became a news photographer. But it has only been since the advent of digital photography that I have ventured beyond the hobbyist level. In the old days, one would purchase a roll of film, typically 12, 24, or 36 shots per roll. Once that film was exposed, you would then need to pay for developing the negatives (or transparencies—where the term "slides" came from), which often included small prints of each. Taking it to the next level, enlarging the image or using it in another venue such as greeting cards, involved sending the image to a laboratory and paying them. You, the photographer, had no control over the final product. Unless you happened to shoot black-and-white and had processing equipment, you were at the mercy of the lab.

With a digital camera and a computer, we today have a plethora of tools and options for manipulating and utilizing our images. You can easily turn an ordinary photo into a work of art. A 32gb card can store over a thousand images and cost just a few dollars. If you so desire you can print images yourself at home, or upload them to a convenient lab in a local store for pickup in a short time.

You can purchase a camera that is filled with a wondrous wealth of options, or just use your cell phone. These days cameras can follow us underwater, in the sky, virtually everywhere we go. This is, truly, the golden age of photography.

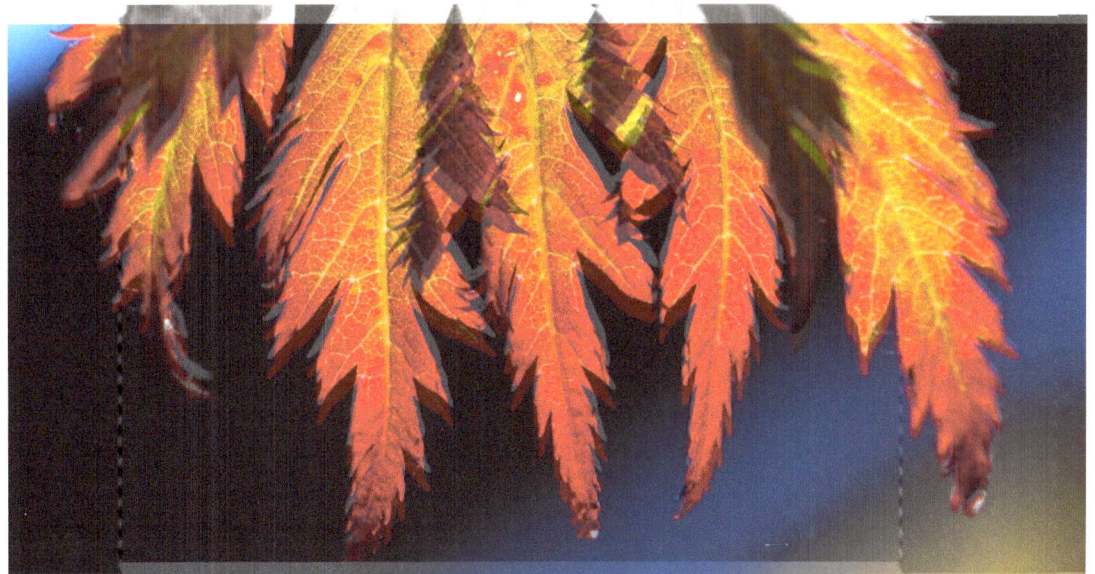

INTRODUCTION

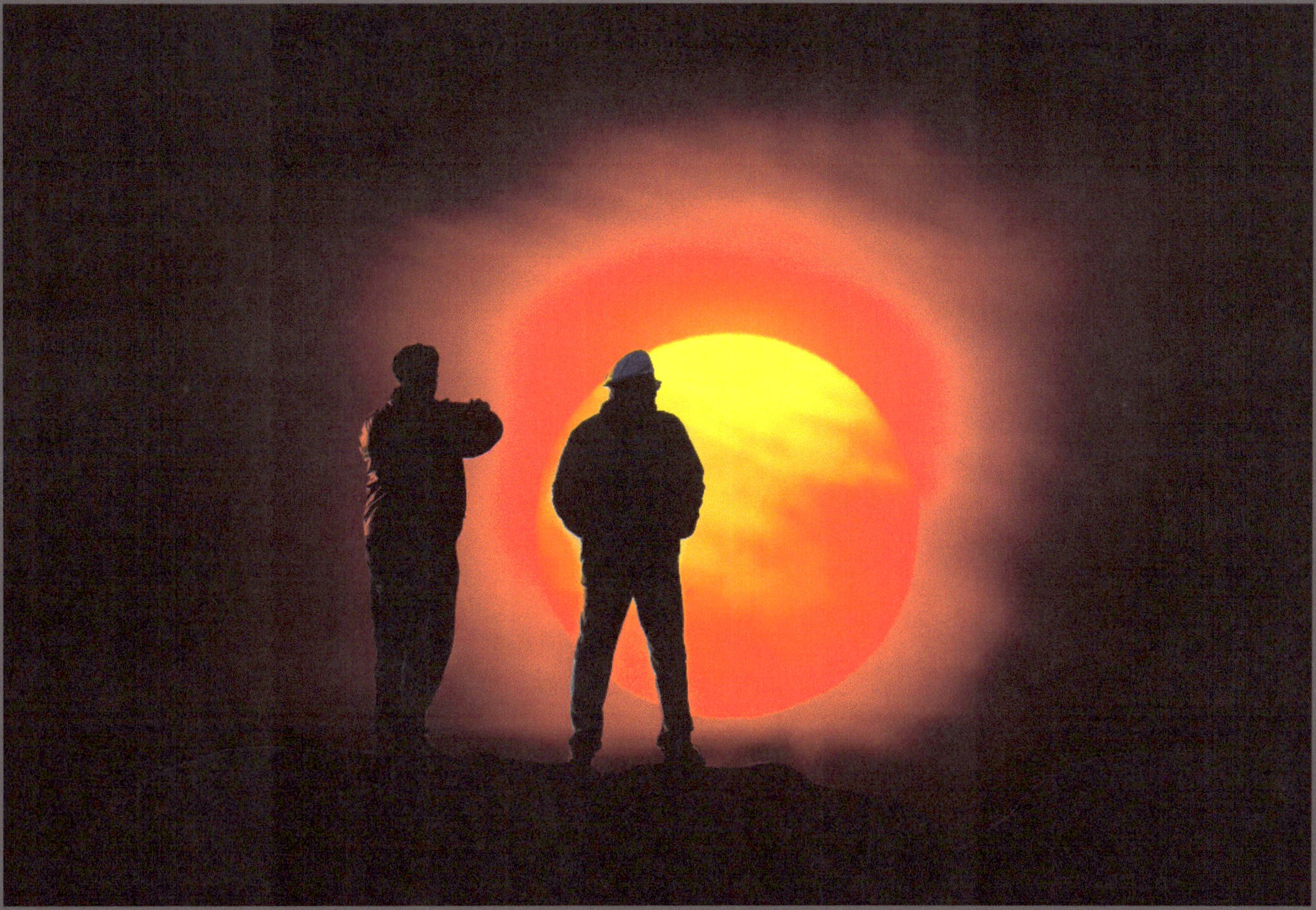

Minding The Sun

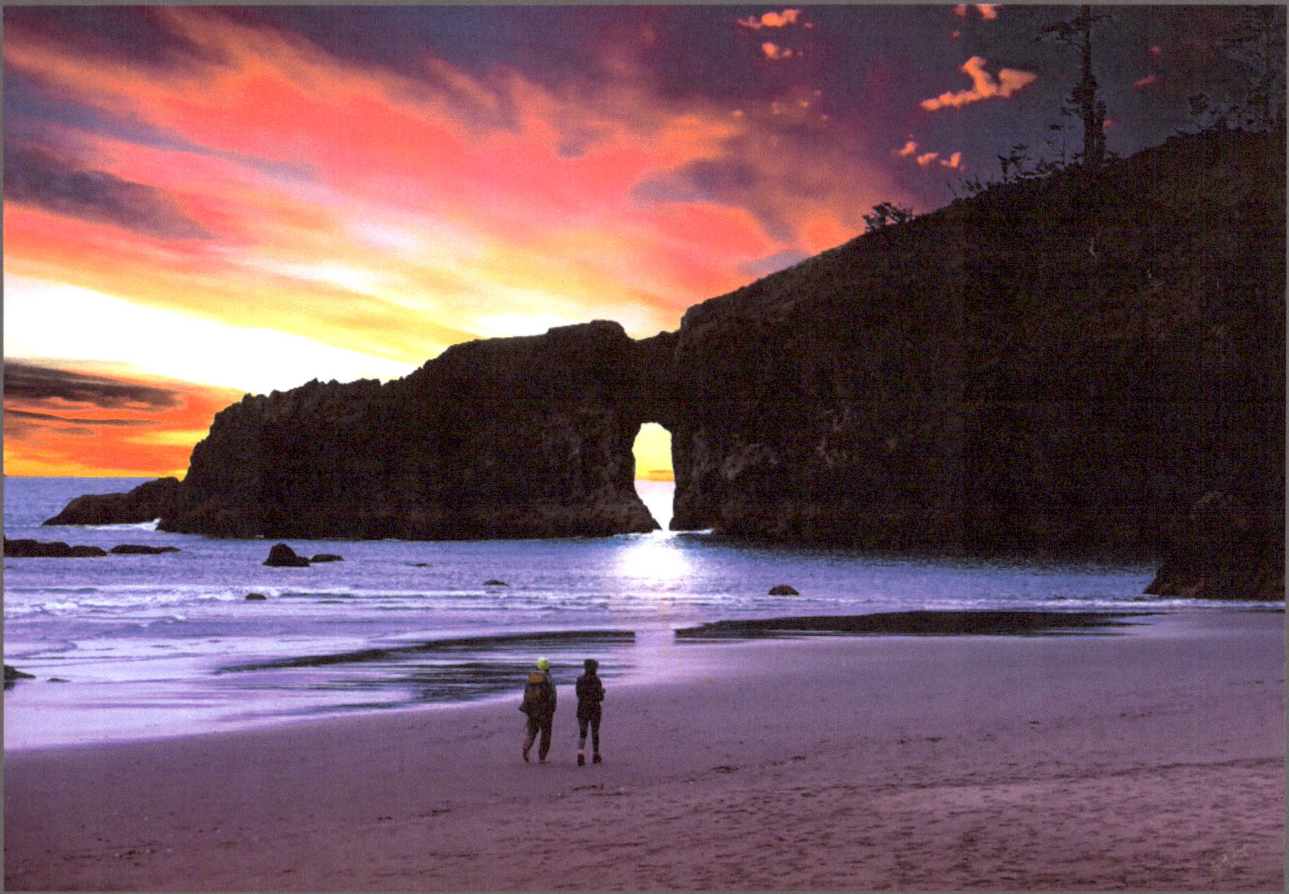

La Push, Washington

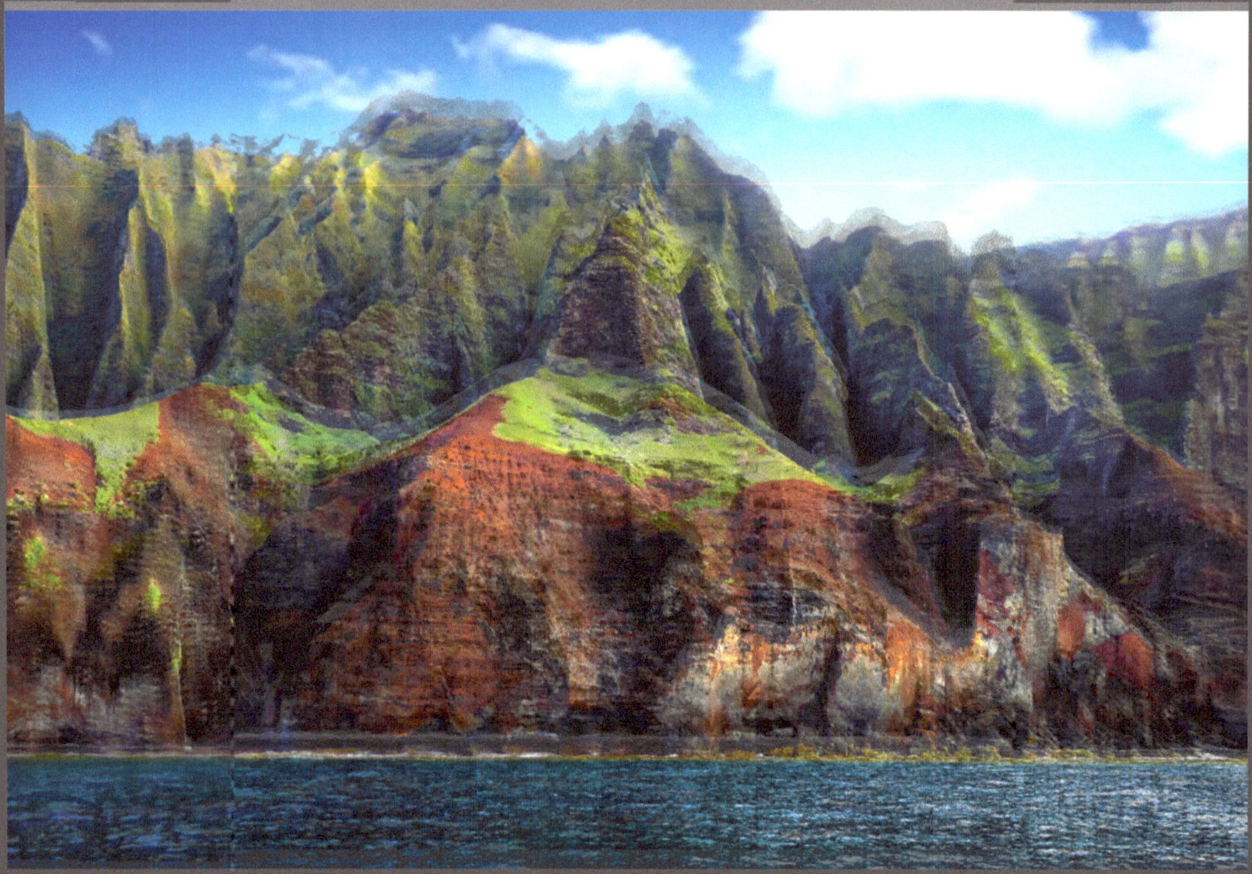

Napali Coast Green

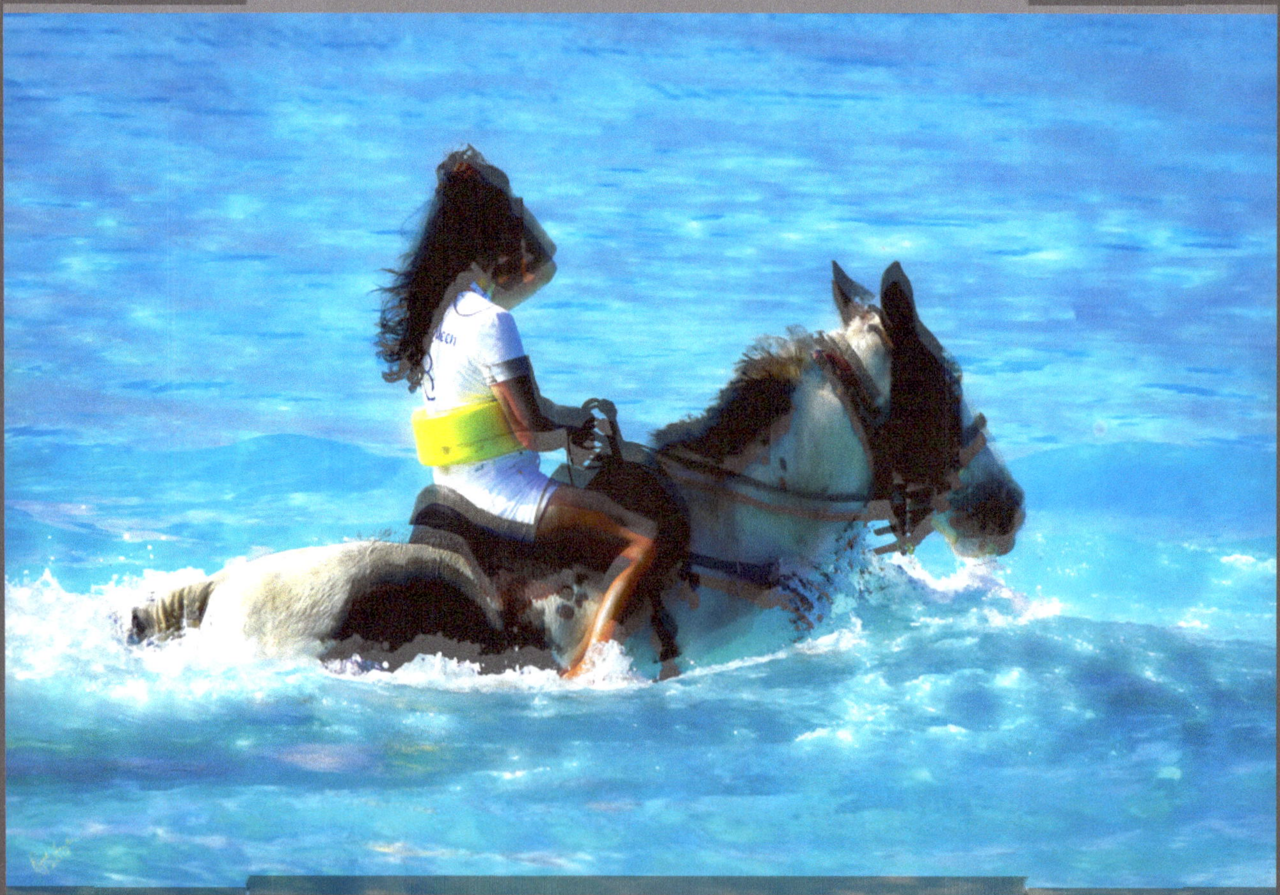

Ride The Dream

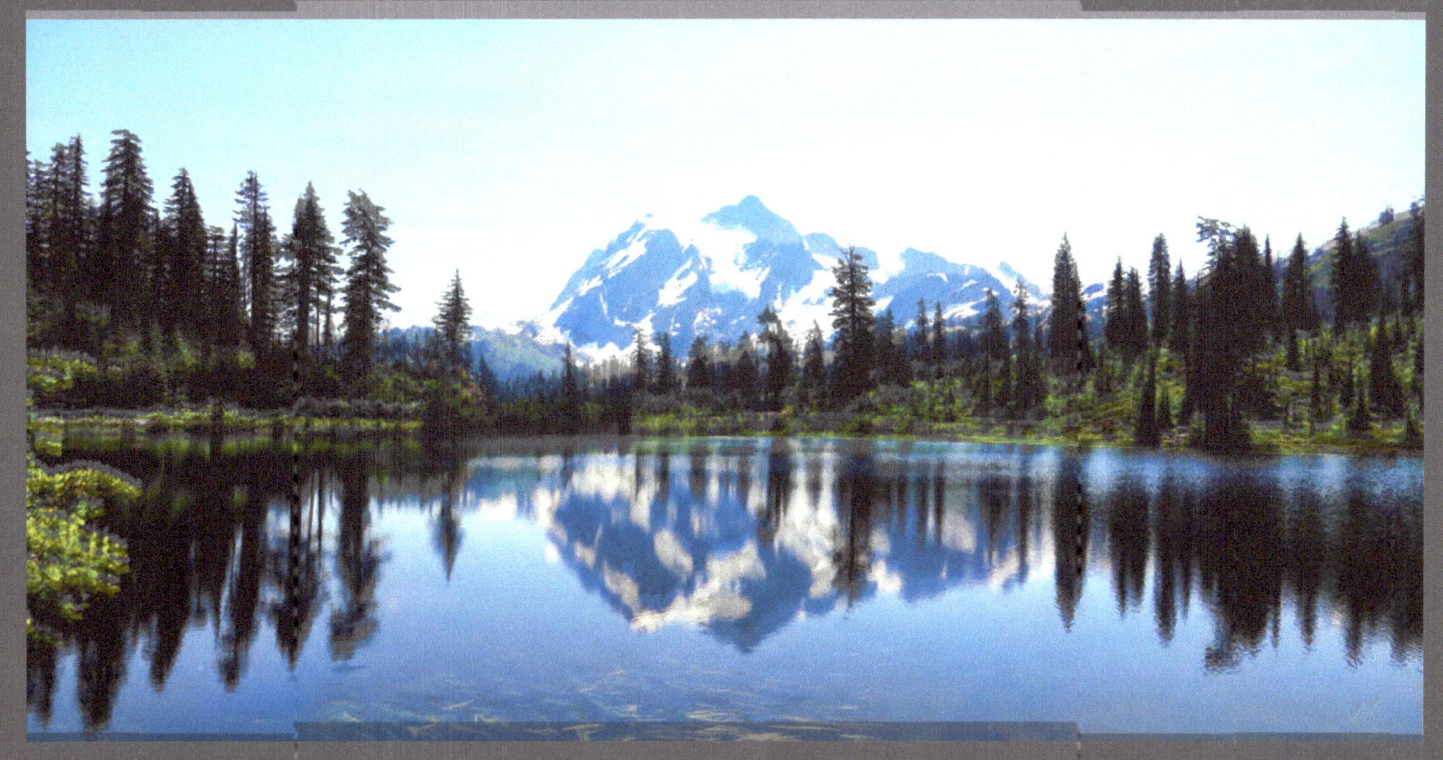

Mt. Shuksan Reflection

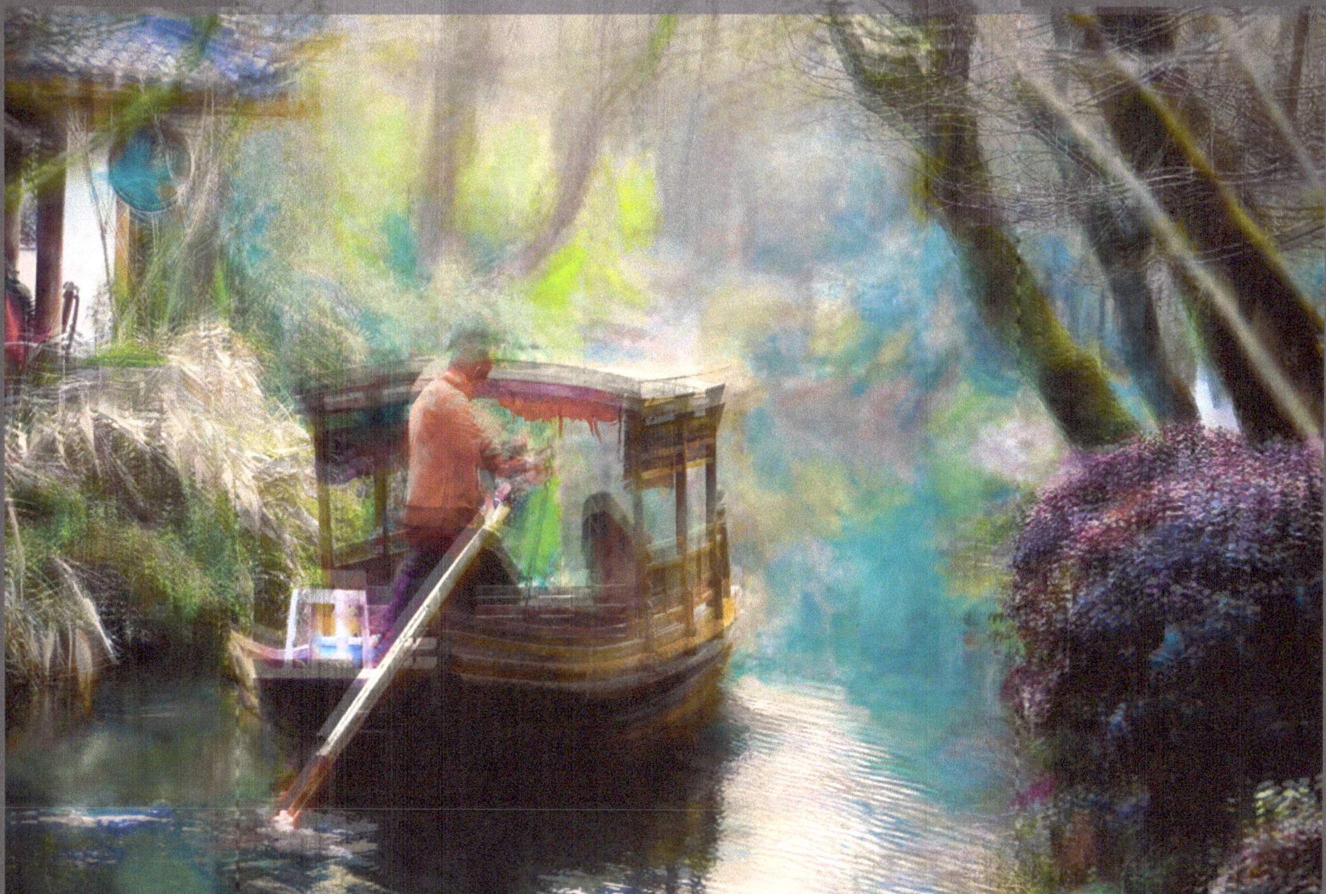

Westlake China

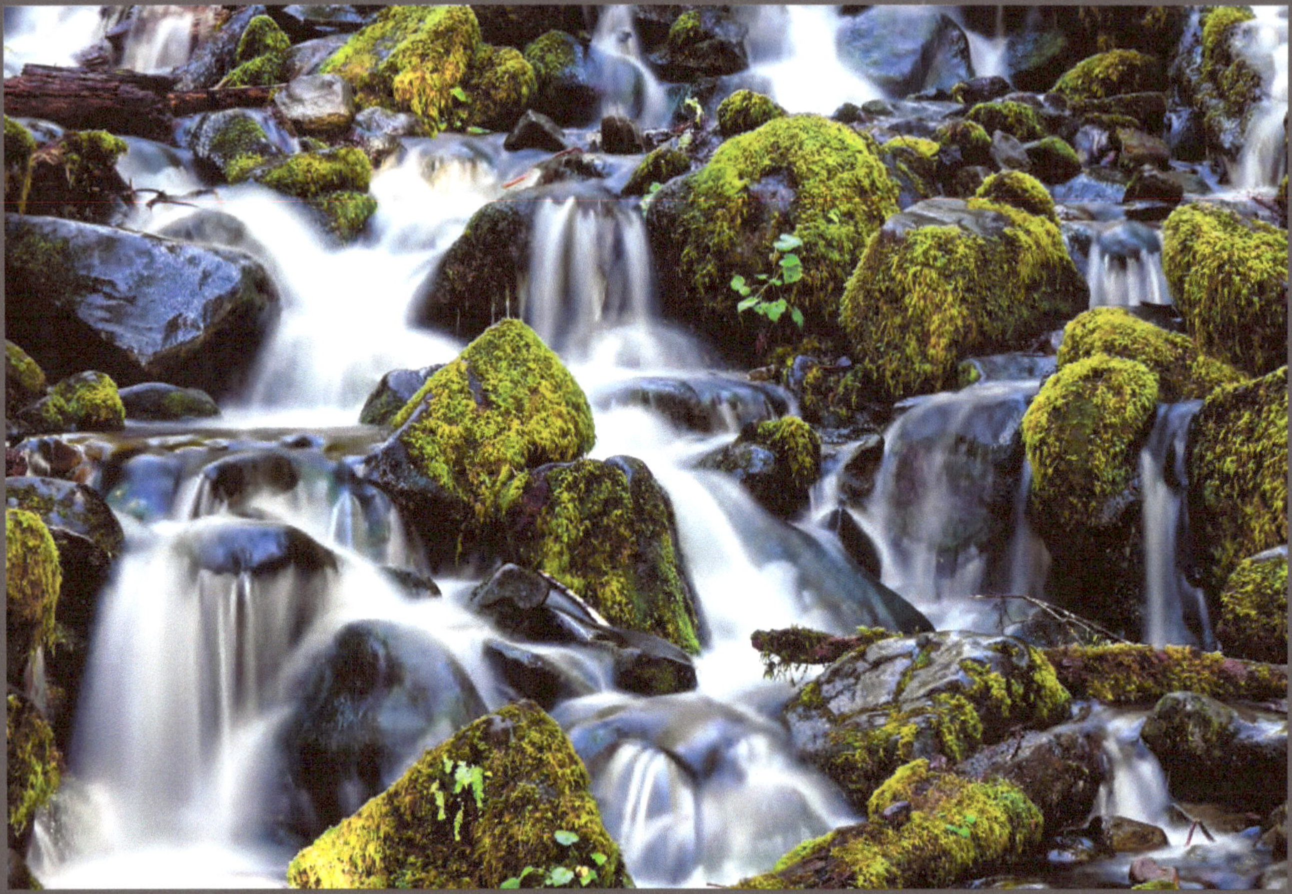

Cascade, Sol Duc Falls

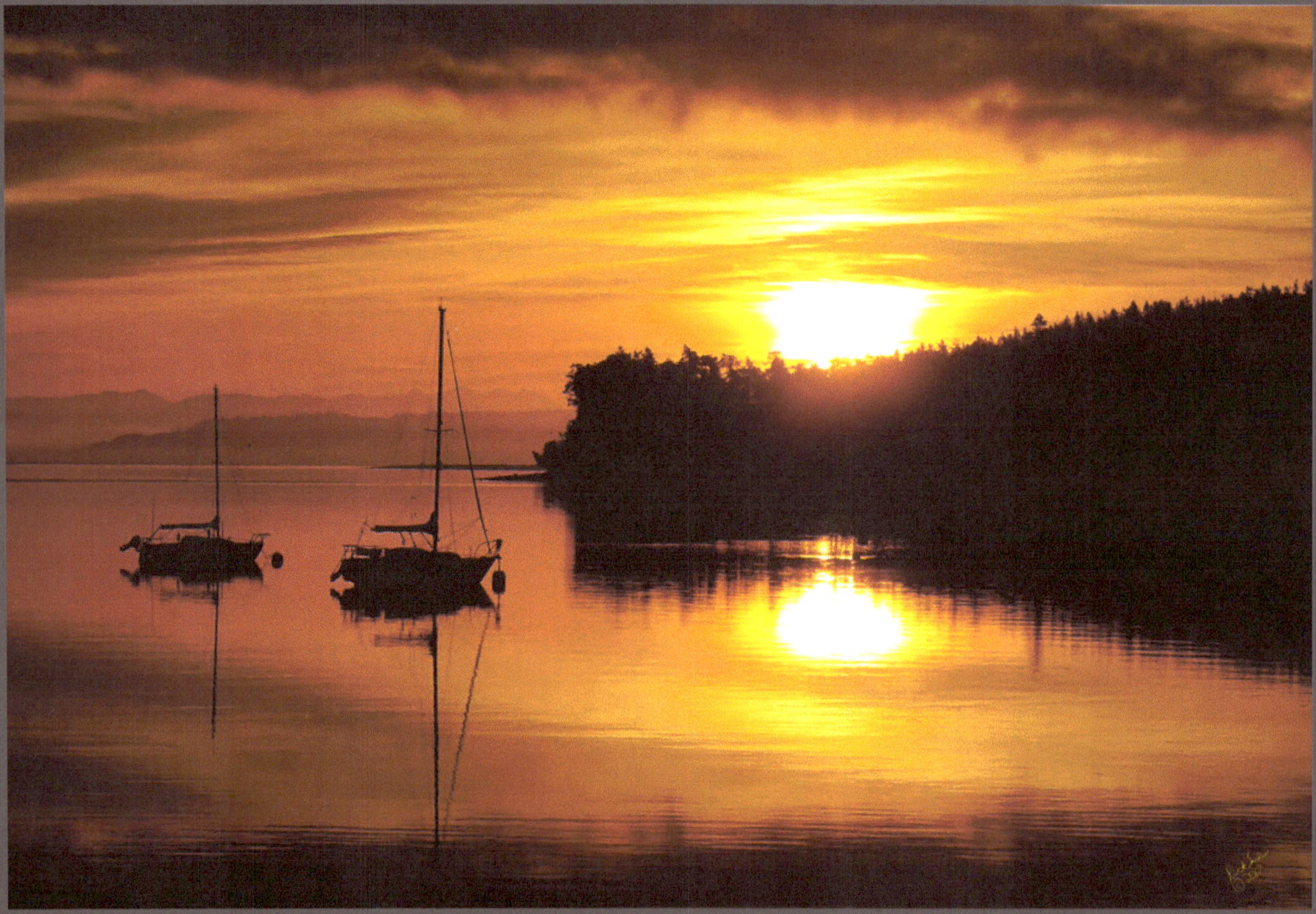

Penn Cove Sunrise

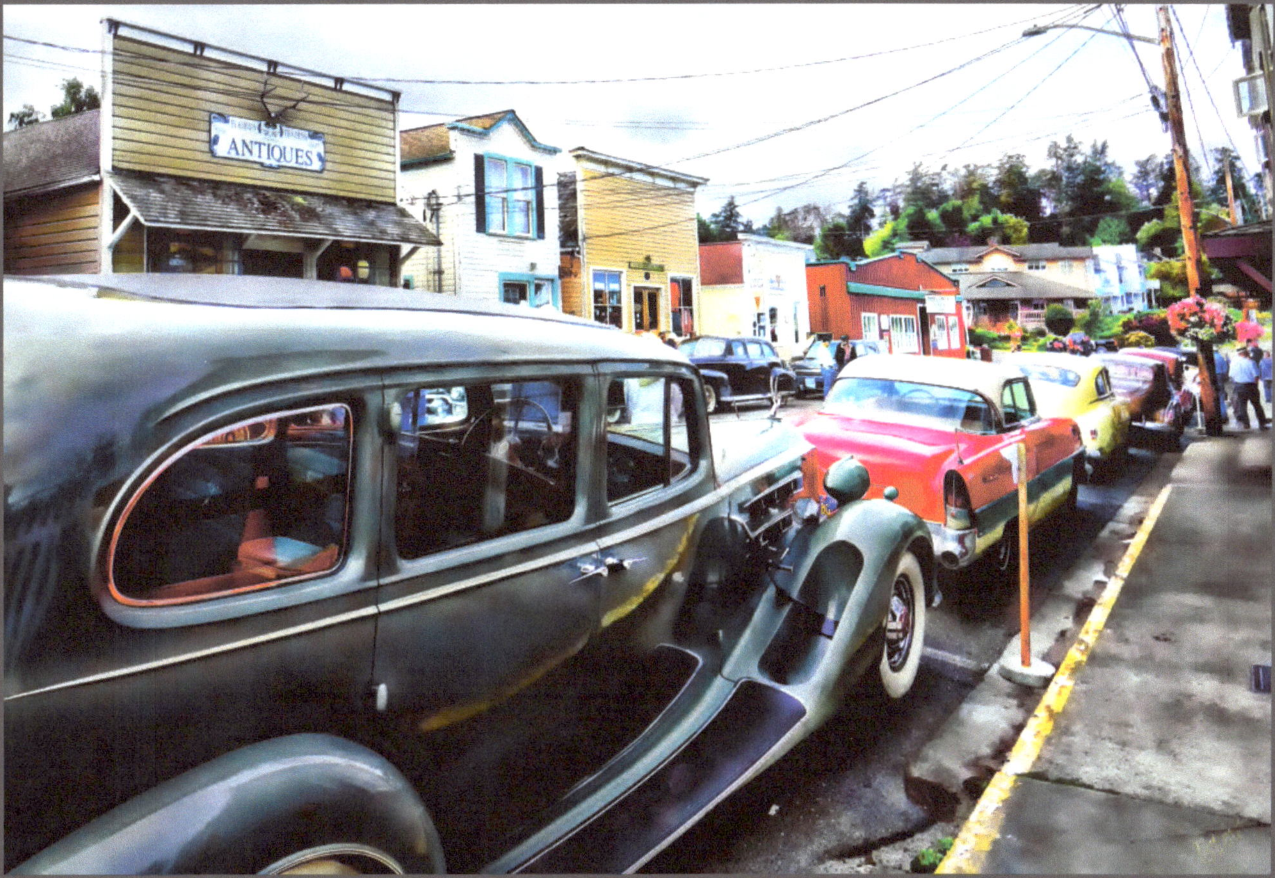

Coupeville Classic Cars

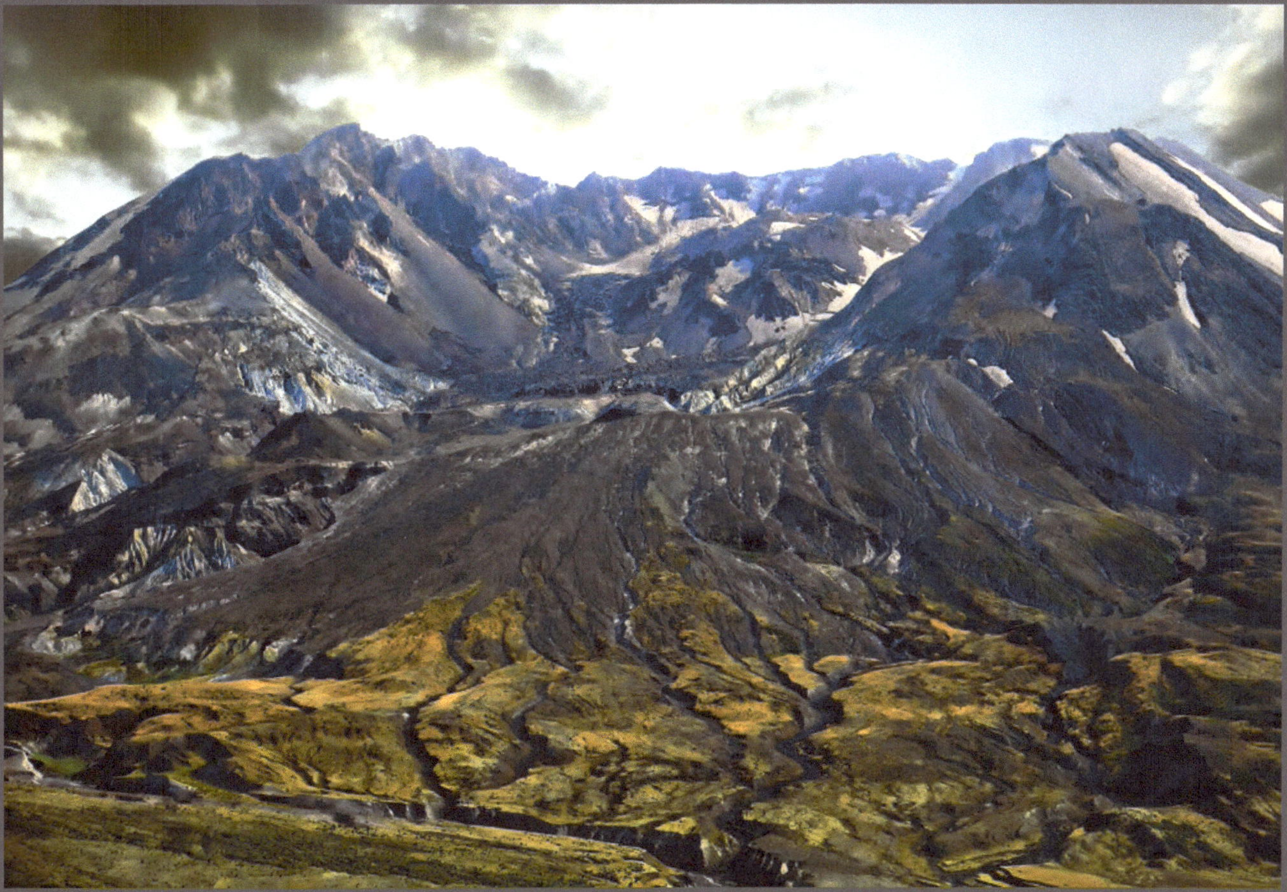

Sleeping Giant

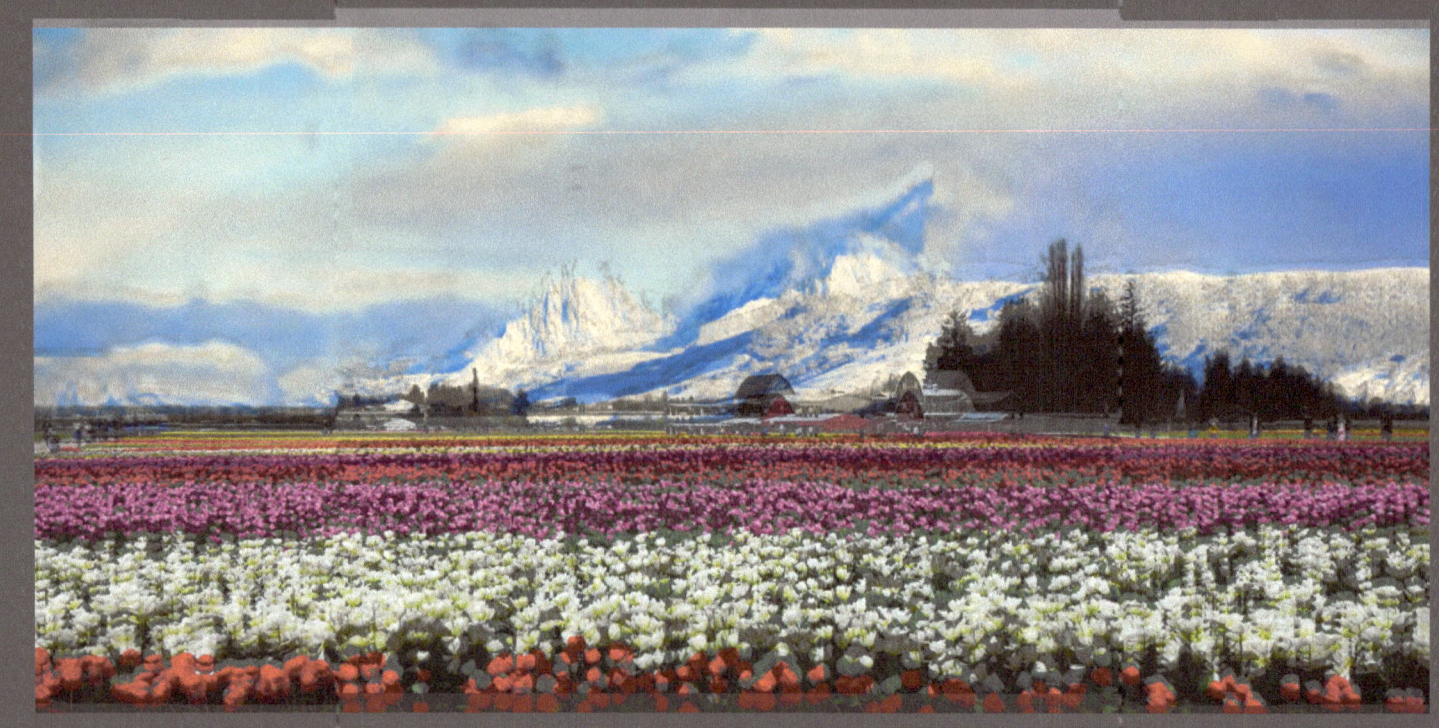

Magic Landscape

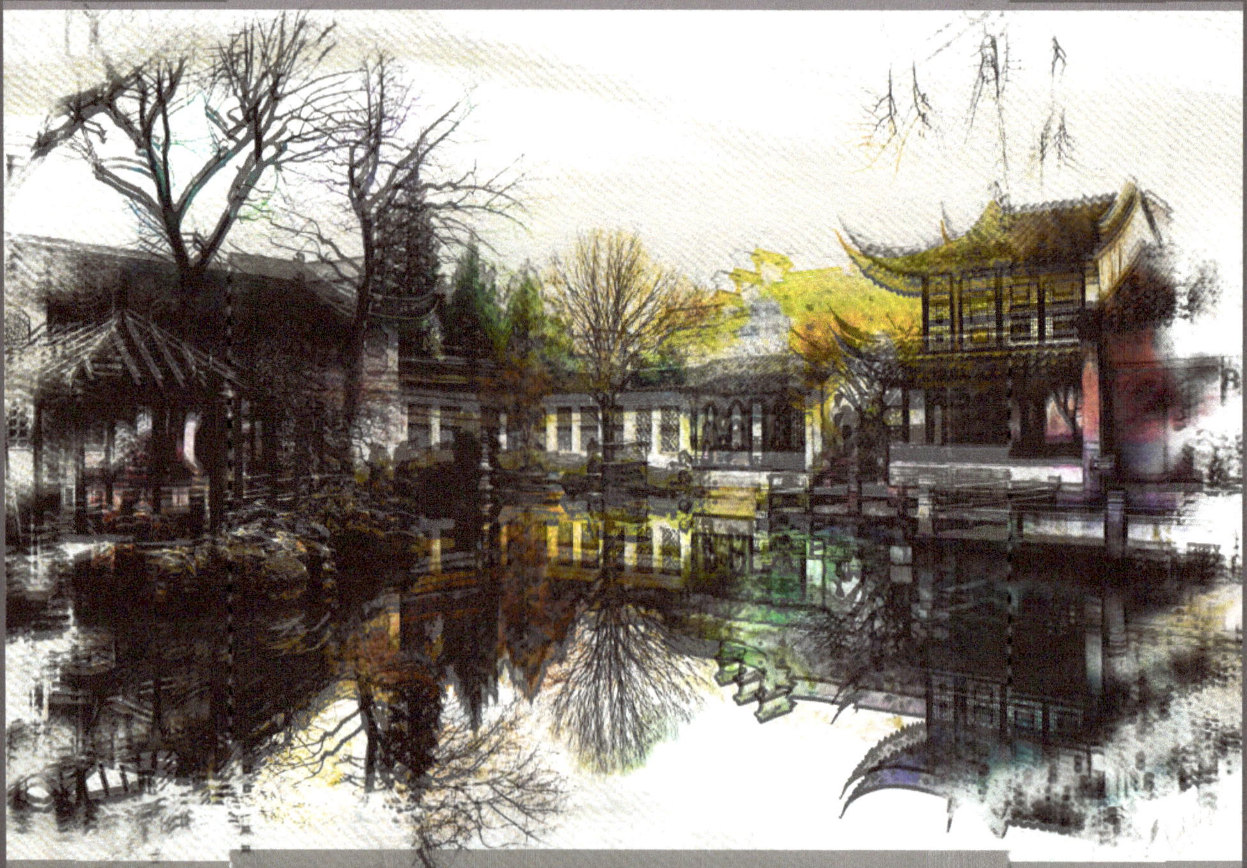

Lingering Garden, China

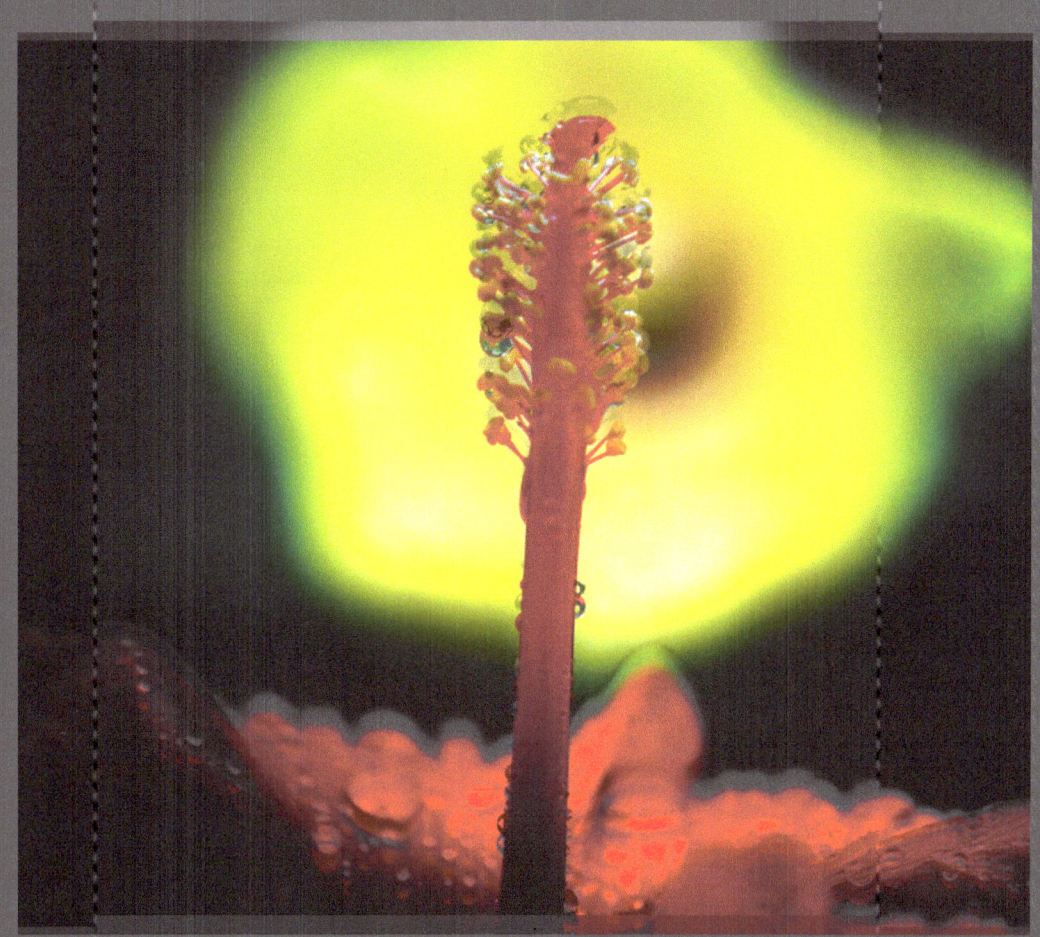

Rain Flower

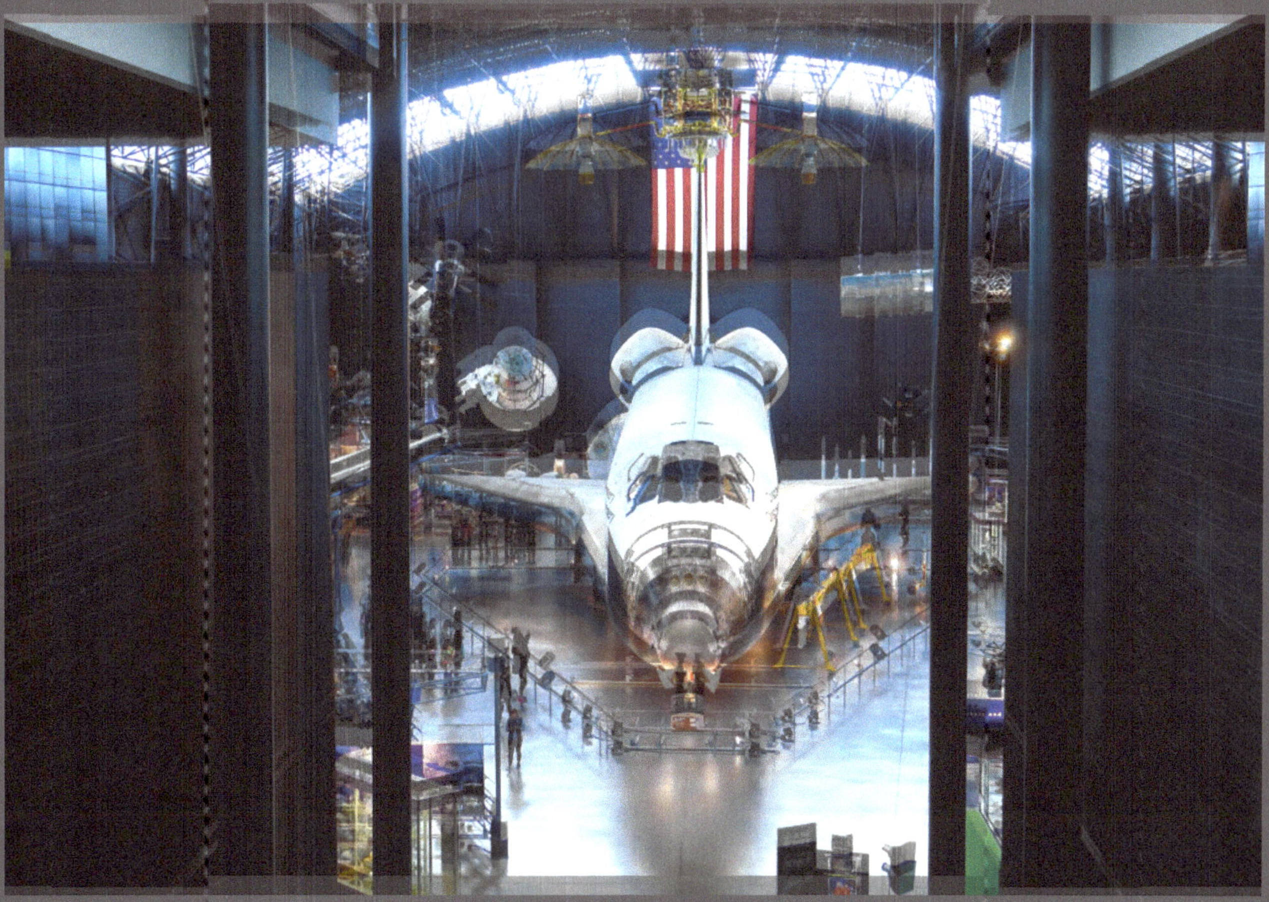

Resting Place

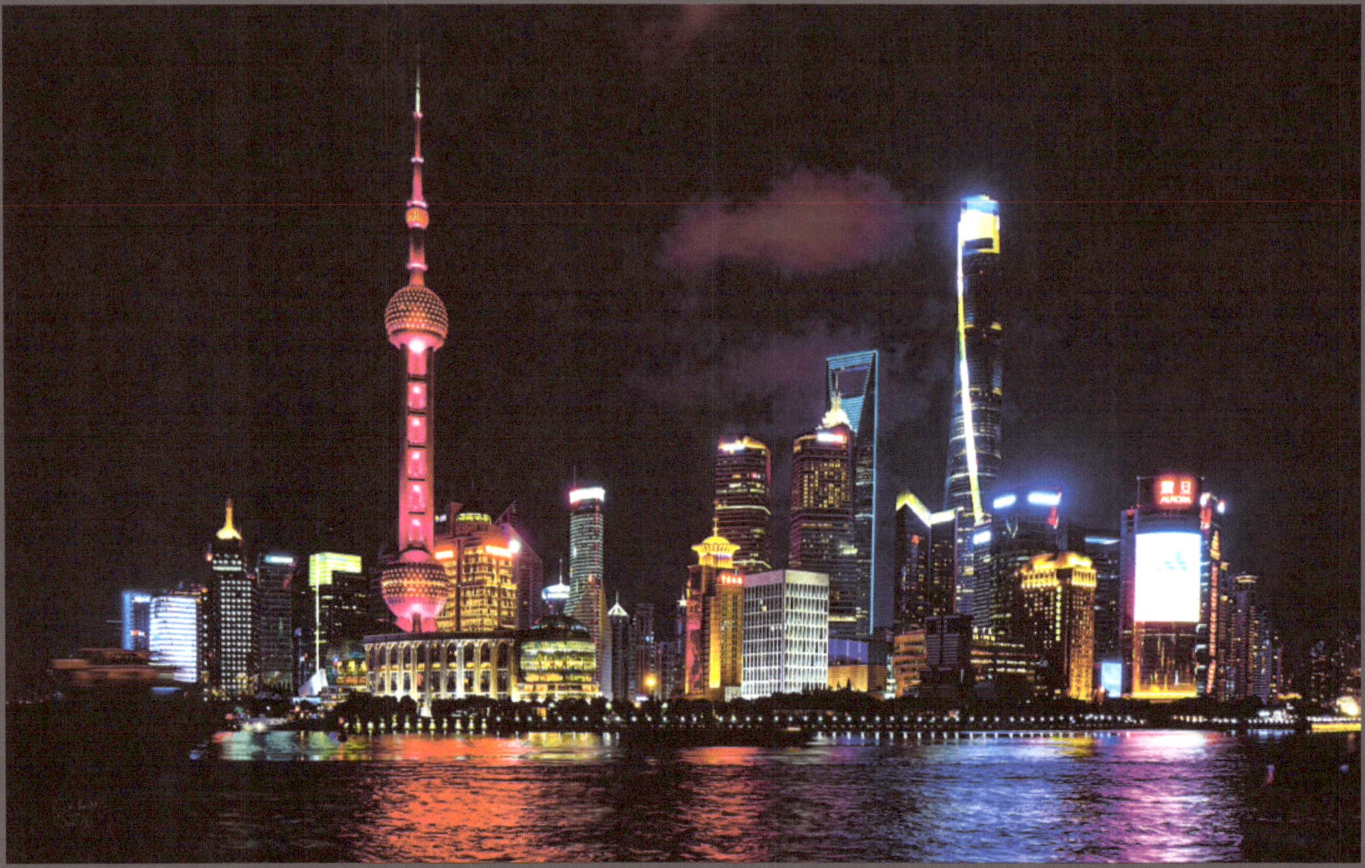

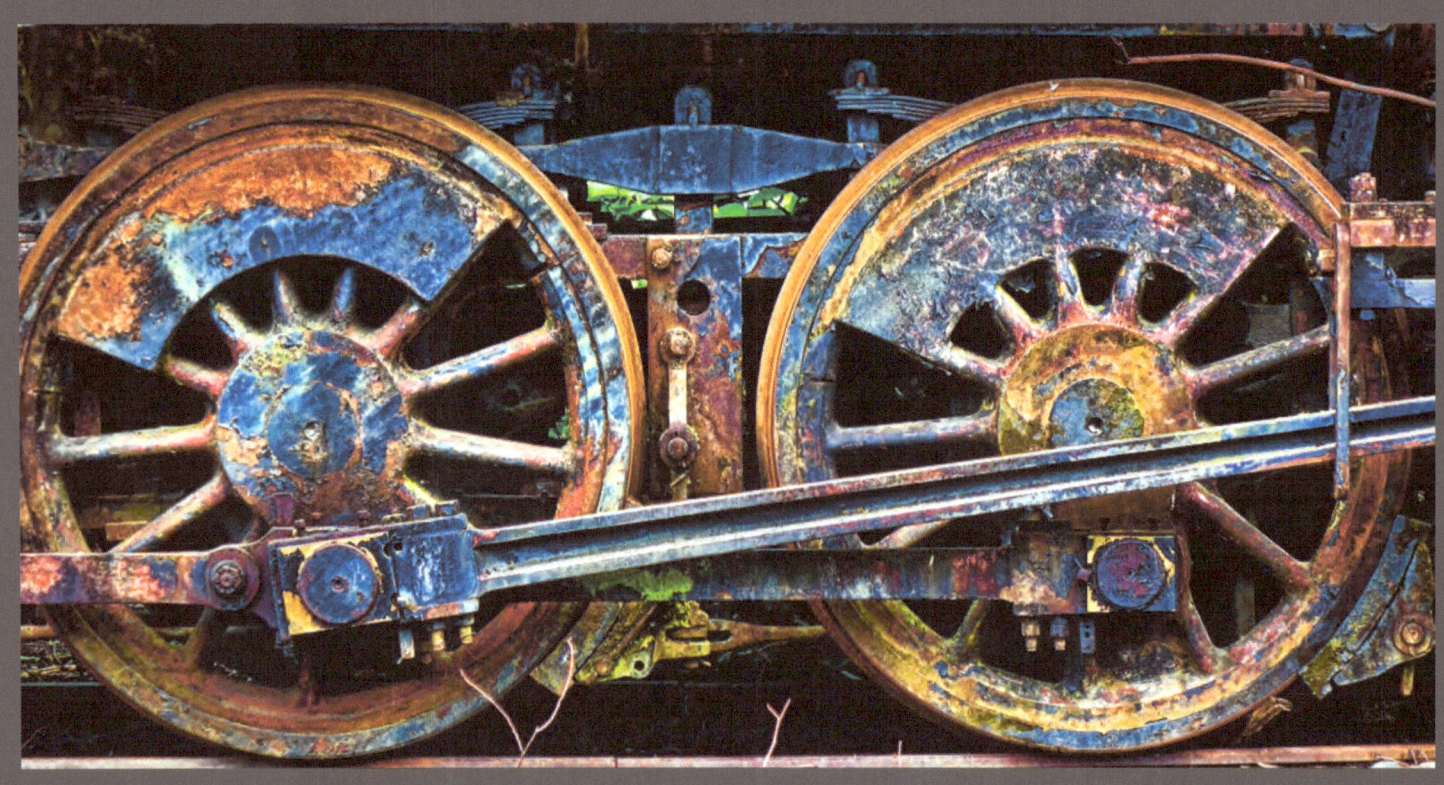

Shanghai at Night

Wheels of Progress

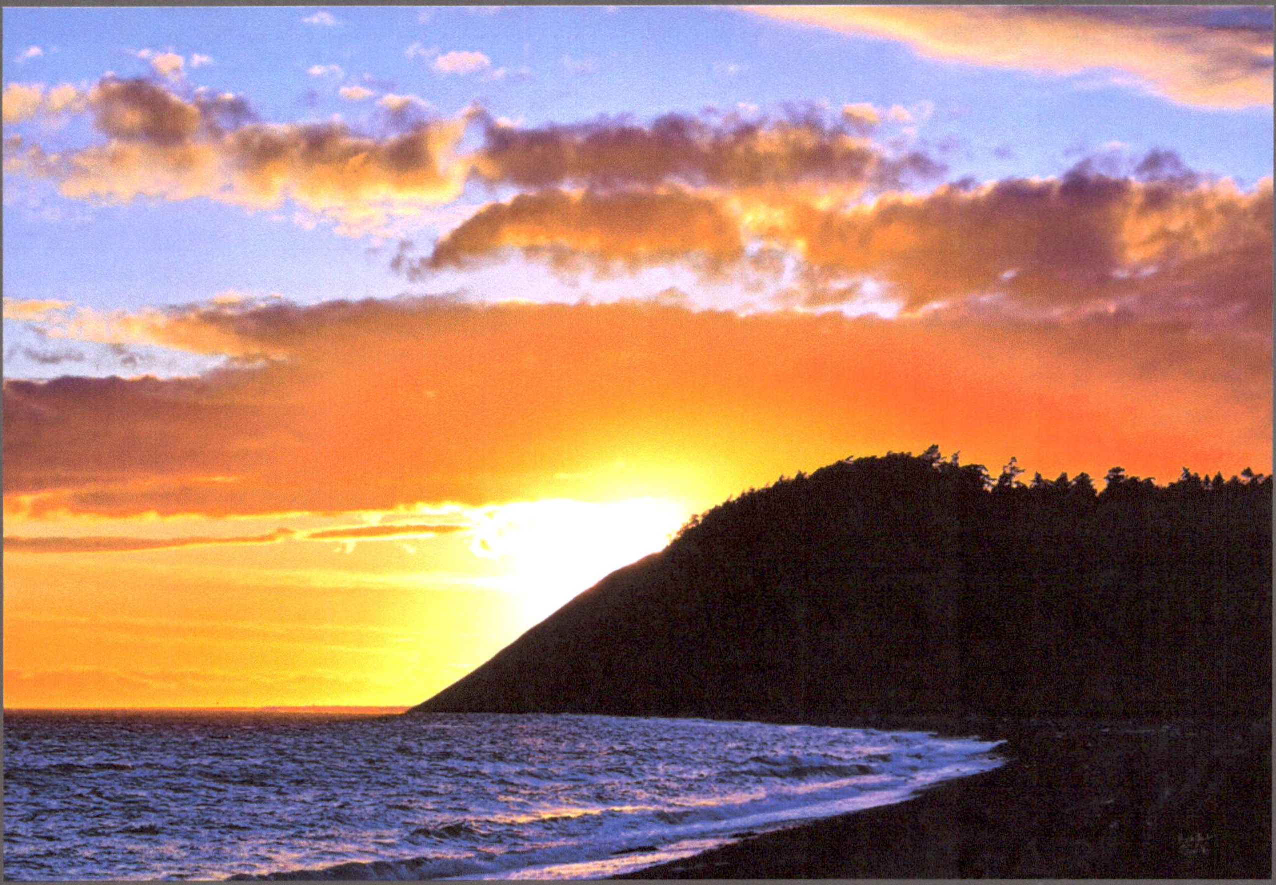

Ebey's Landing Sunset

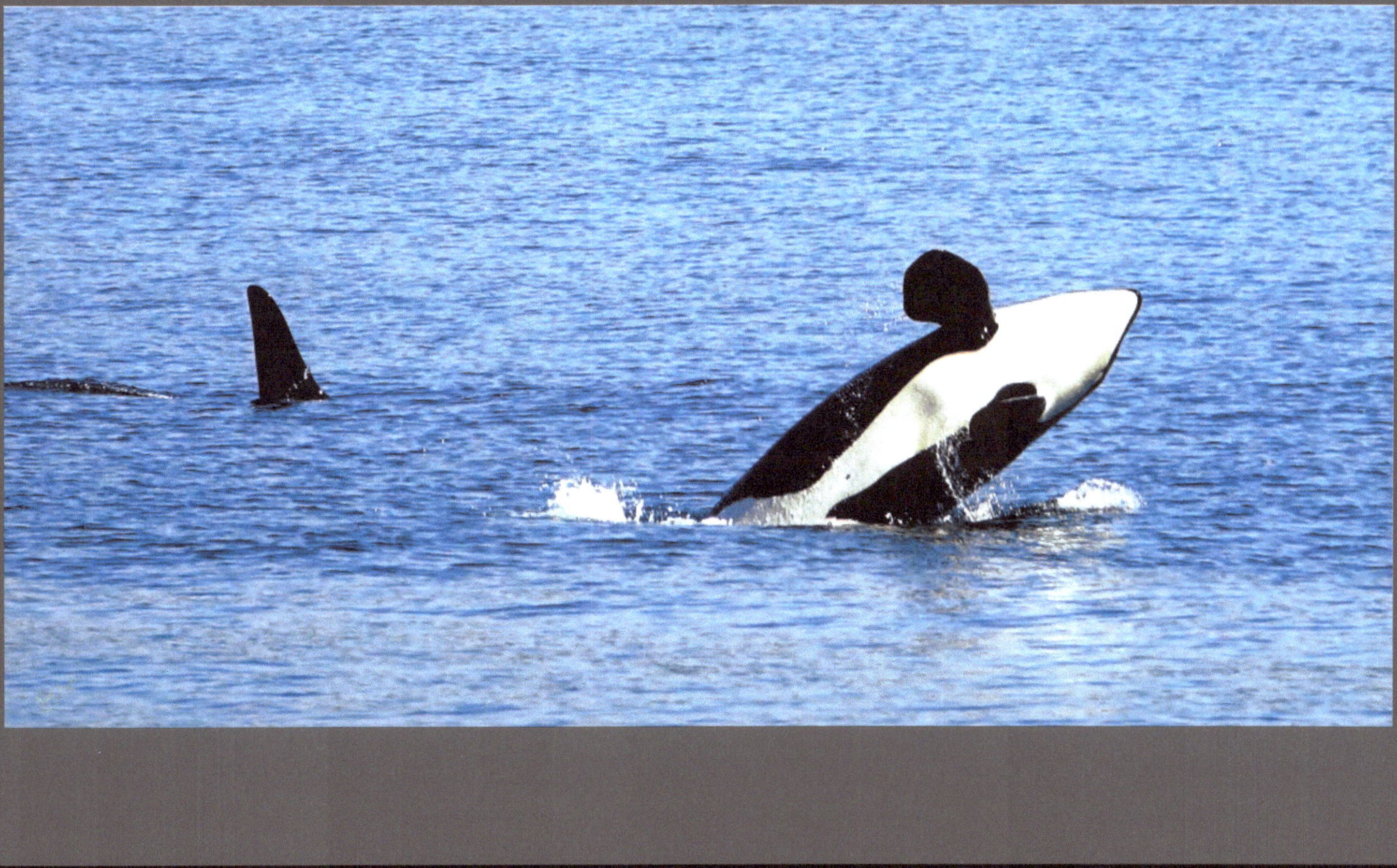

L Pod Leap

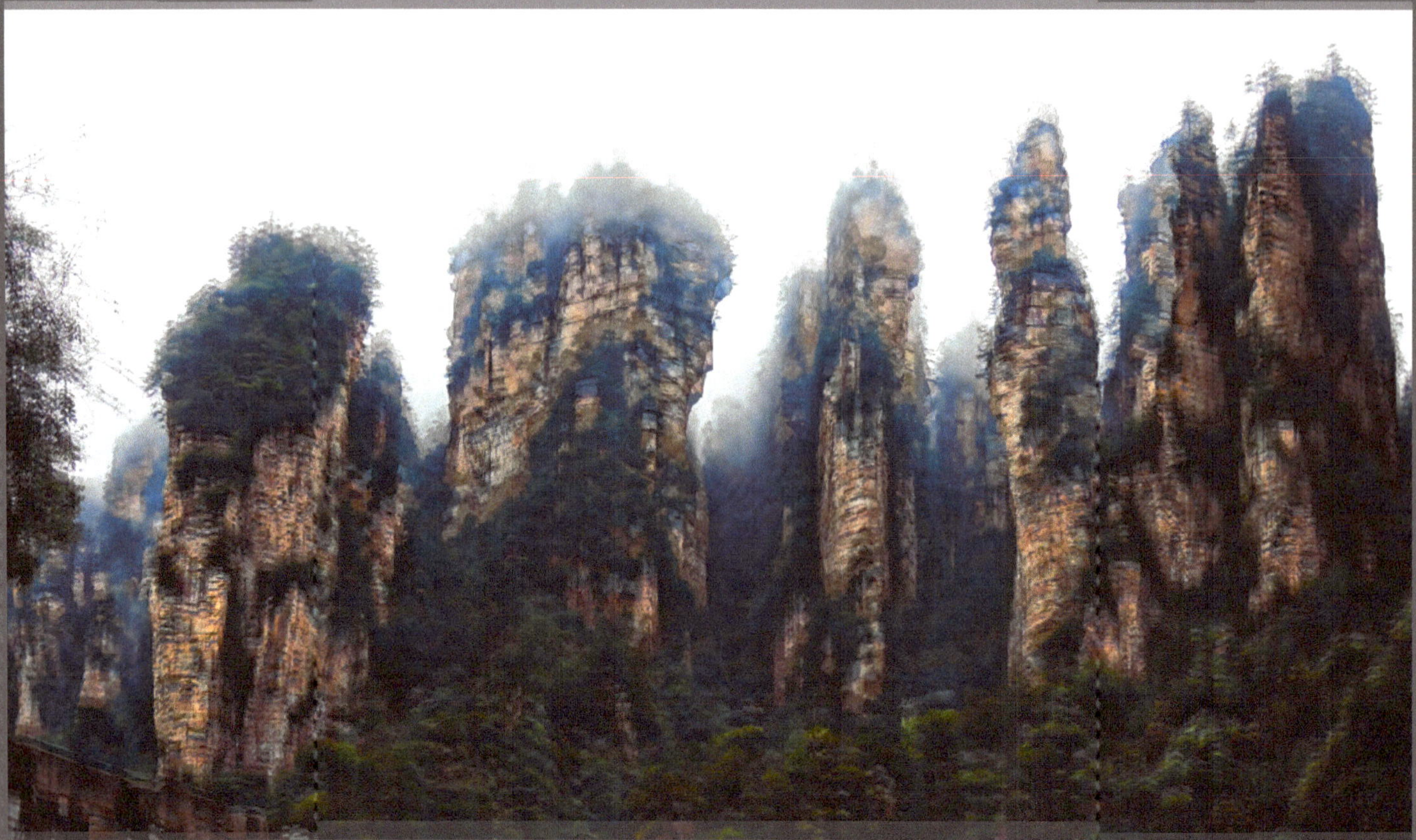

Avatar Mountains

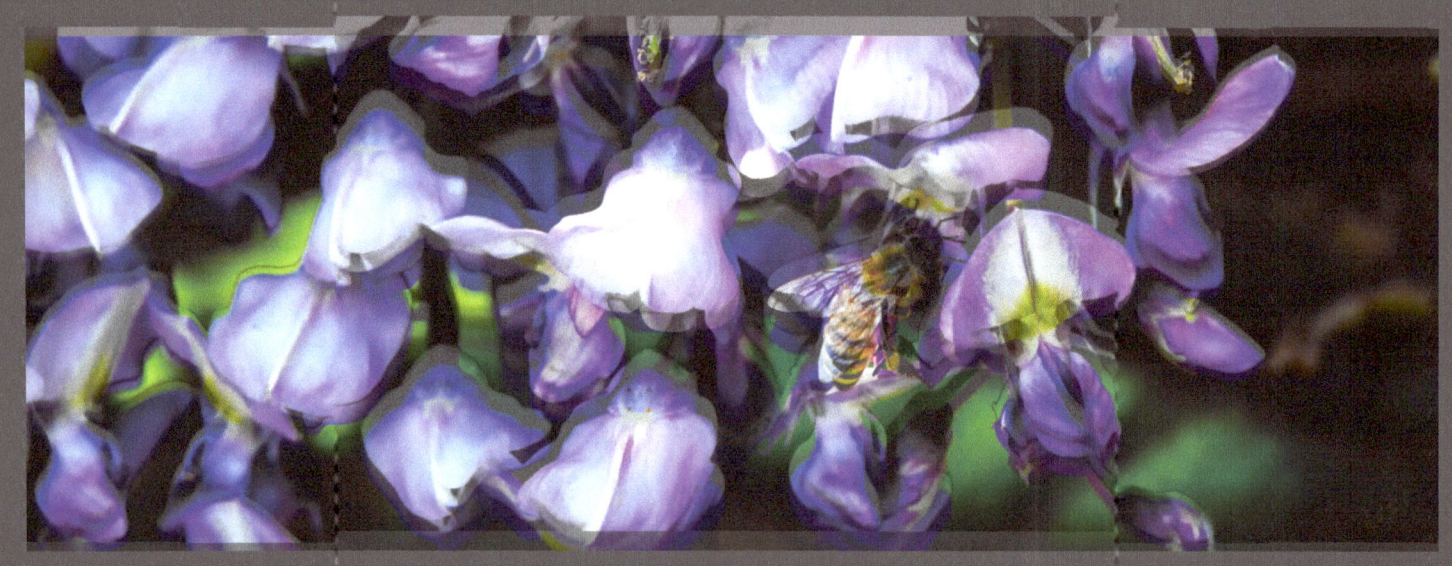

Wysteria Bee

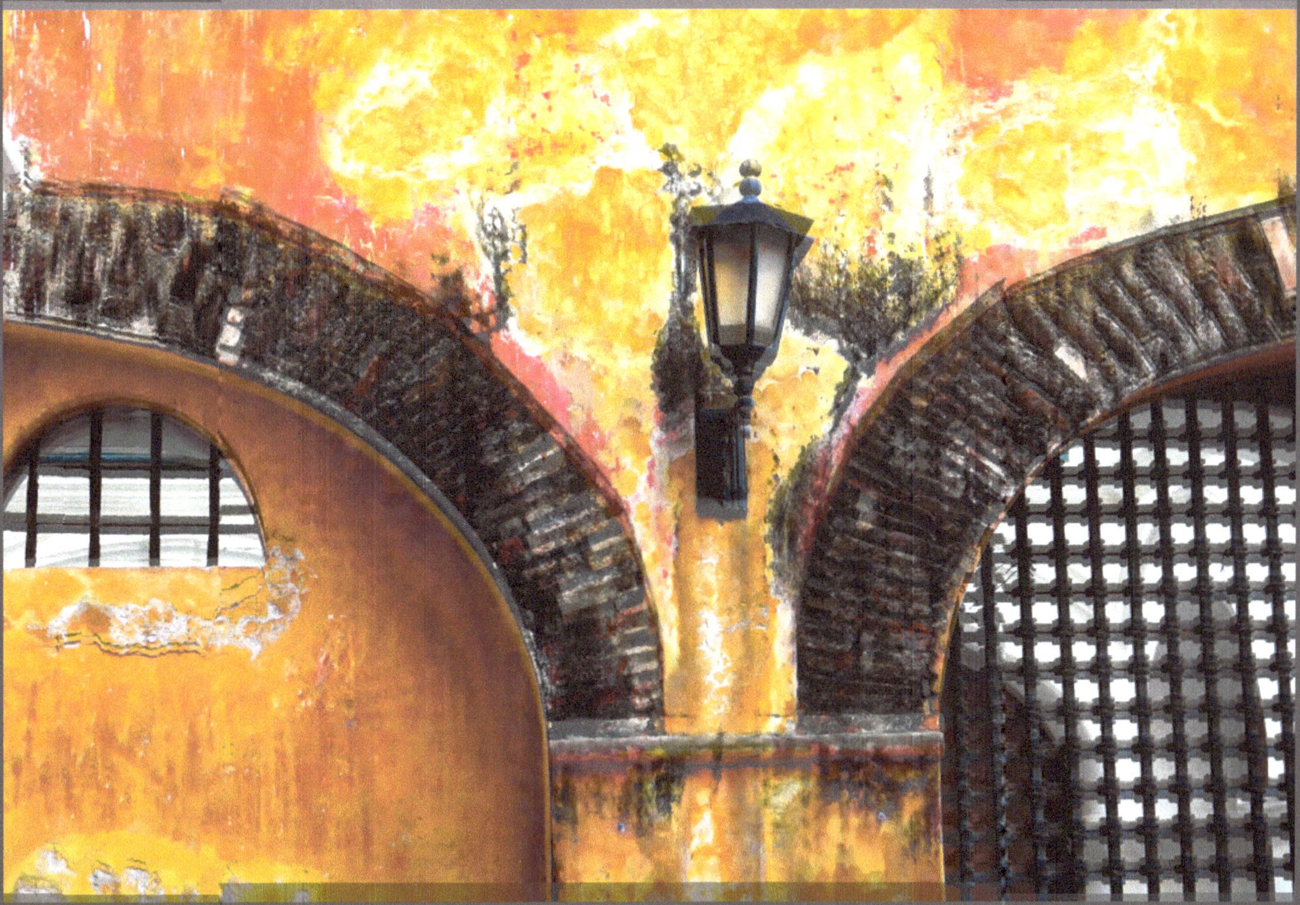

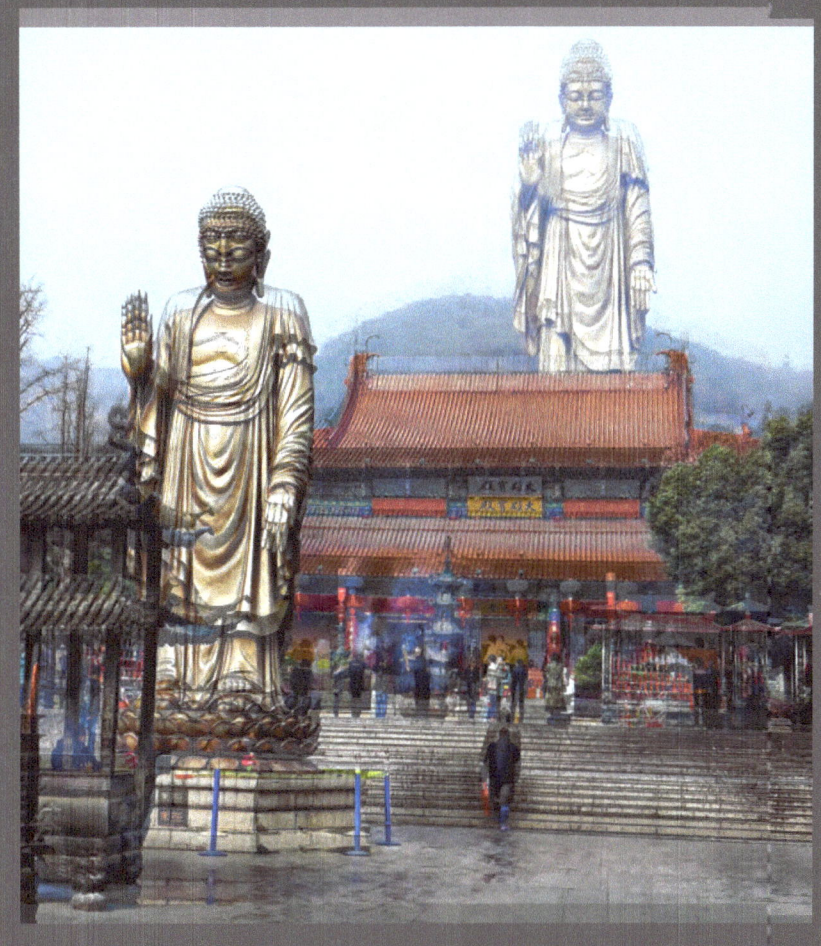

Cartegena Old Town

Lingshan Grand Buddha

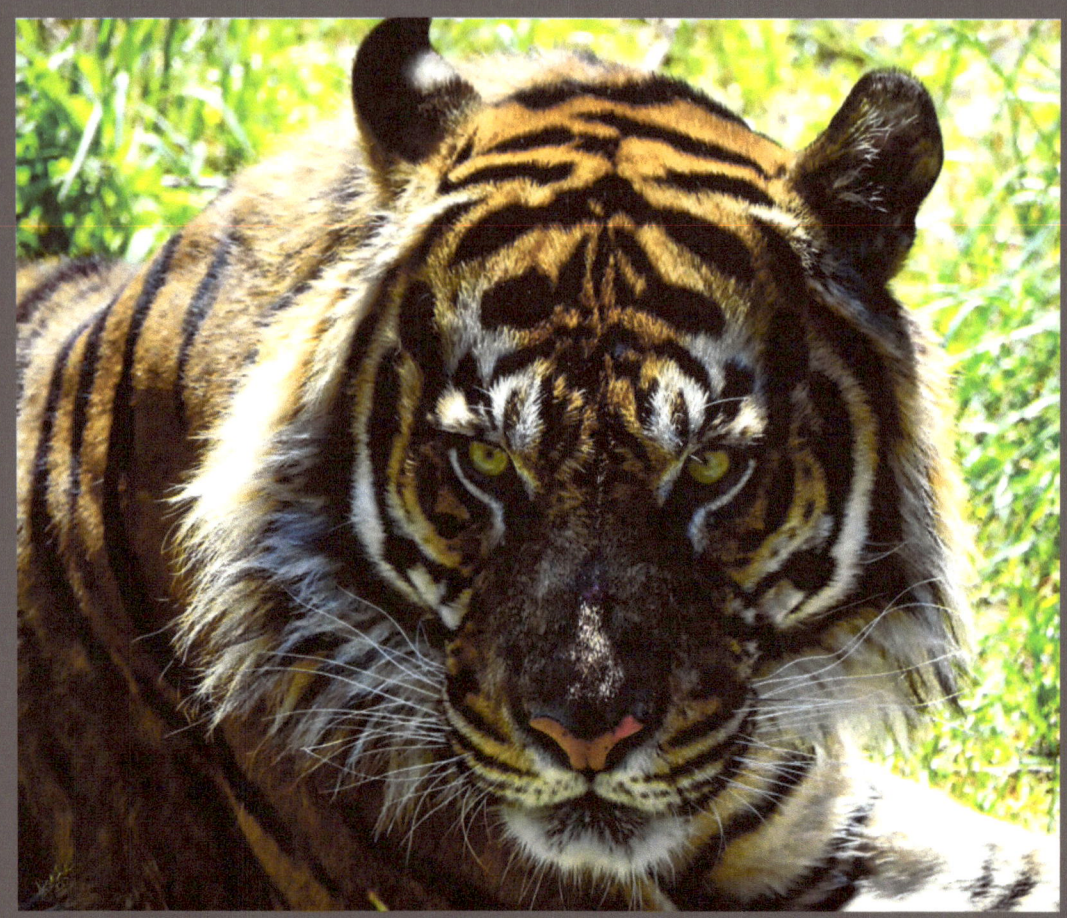

The Stare

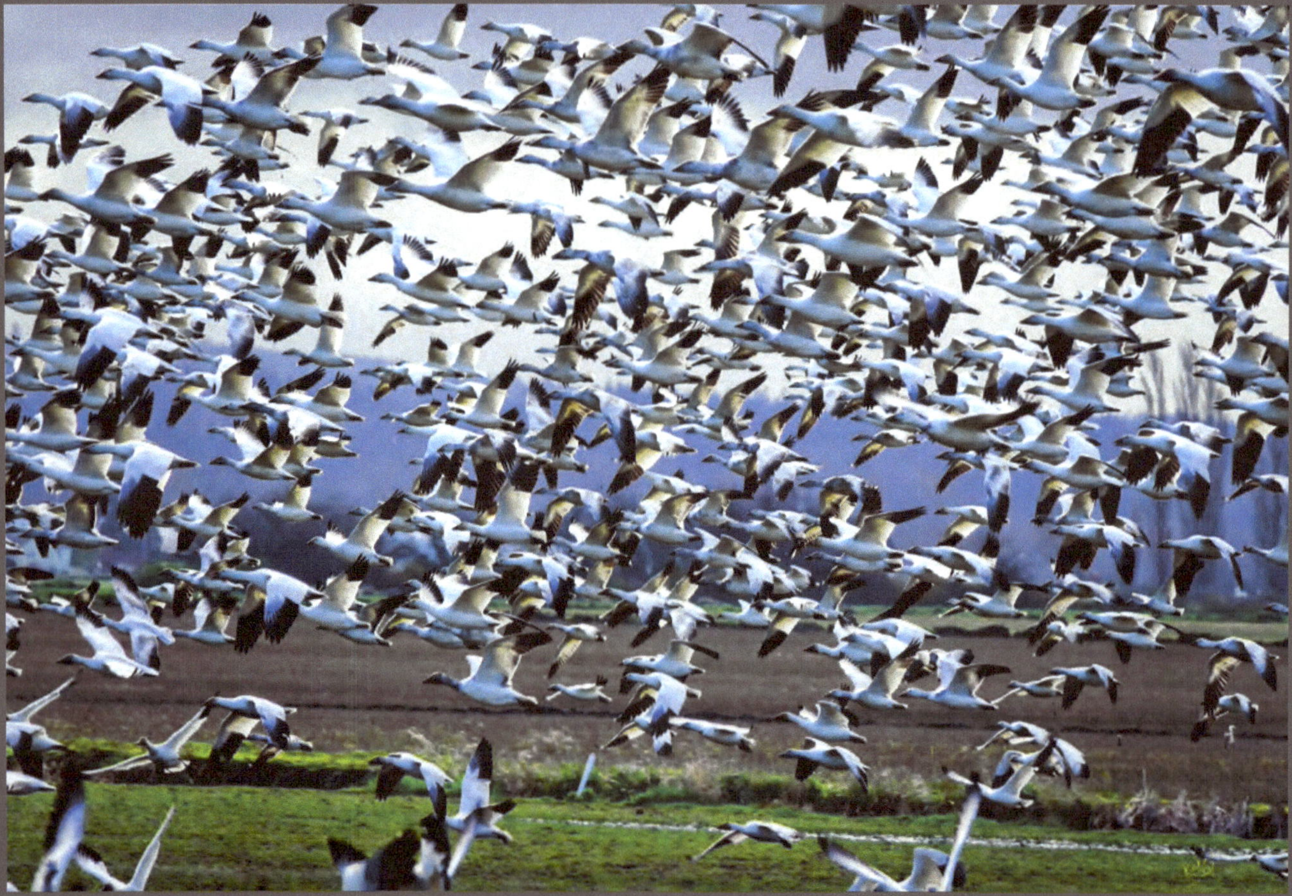

Flight of the Snow Geese

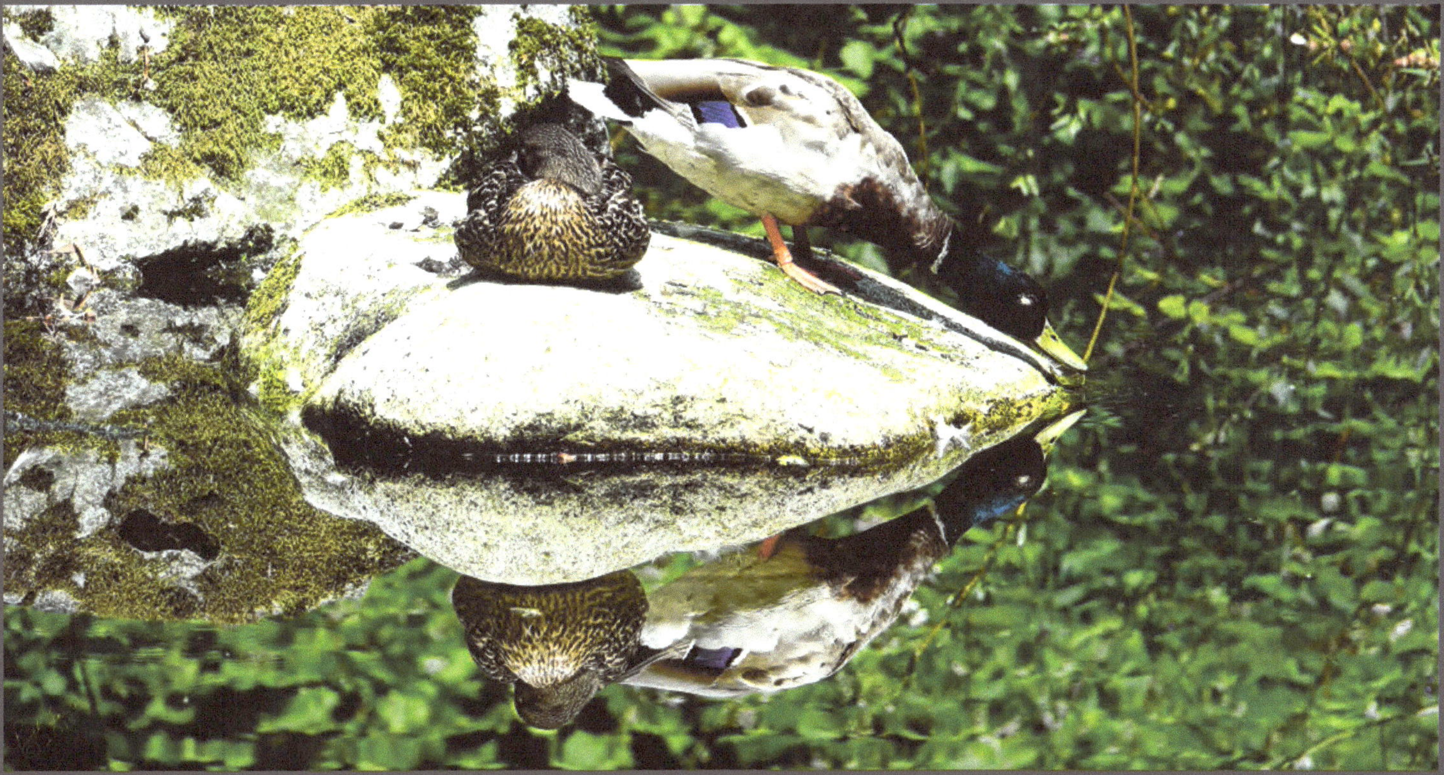

Stanley Park Reflection

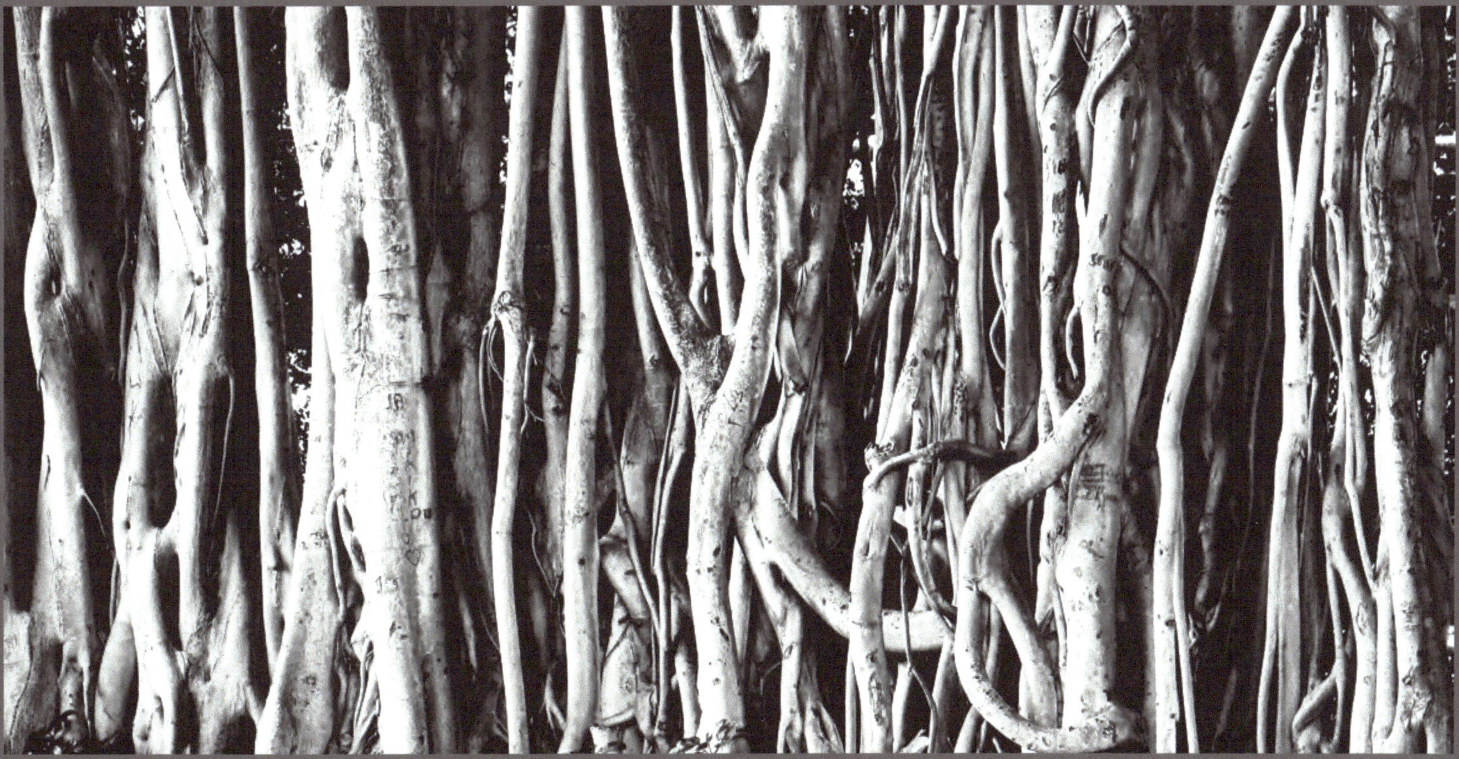

Just A Few Trees

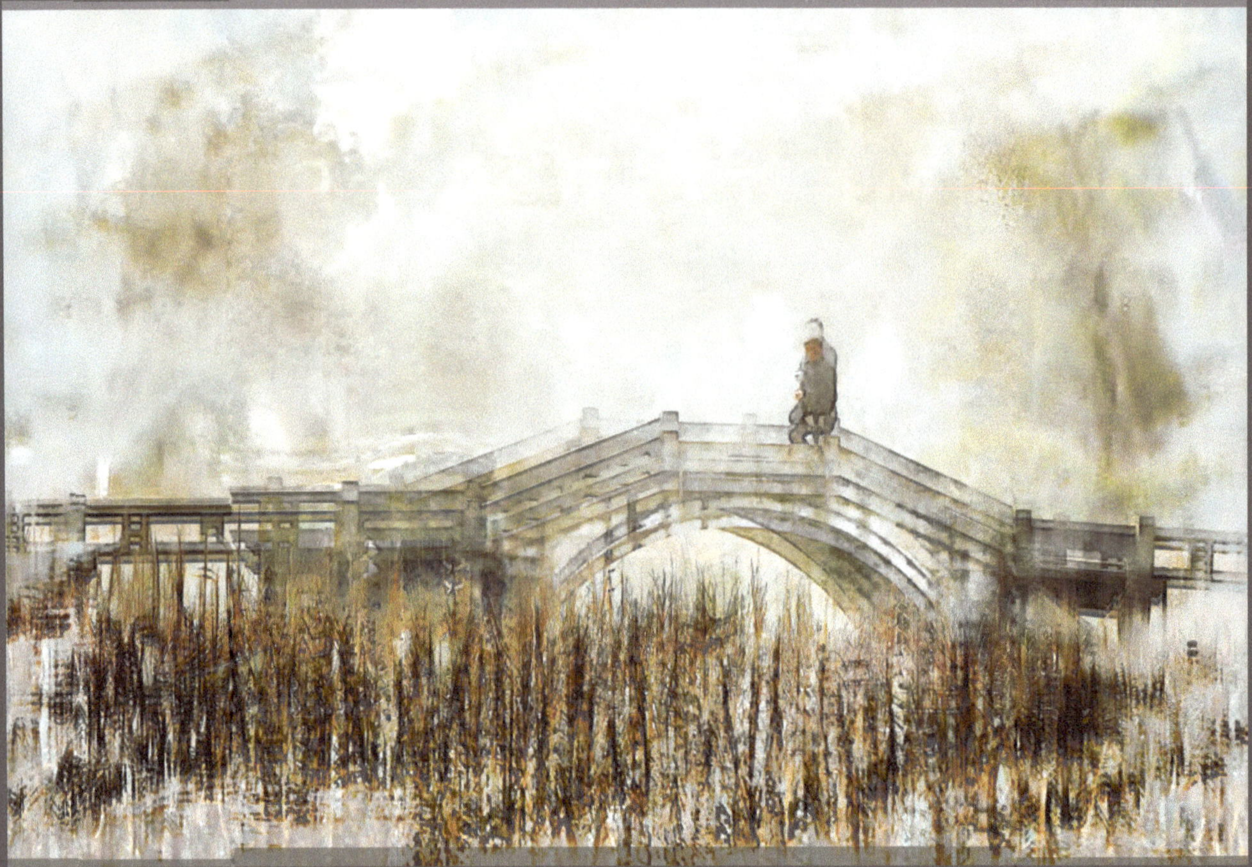

A Bridge, Westlake

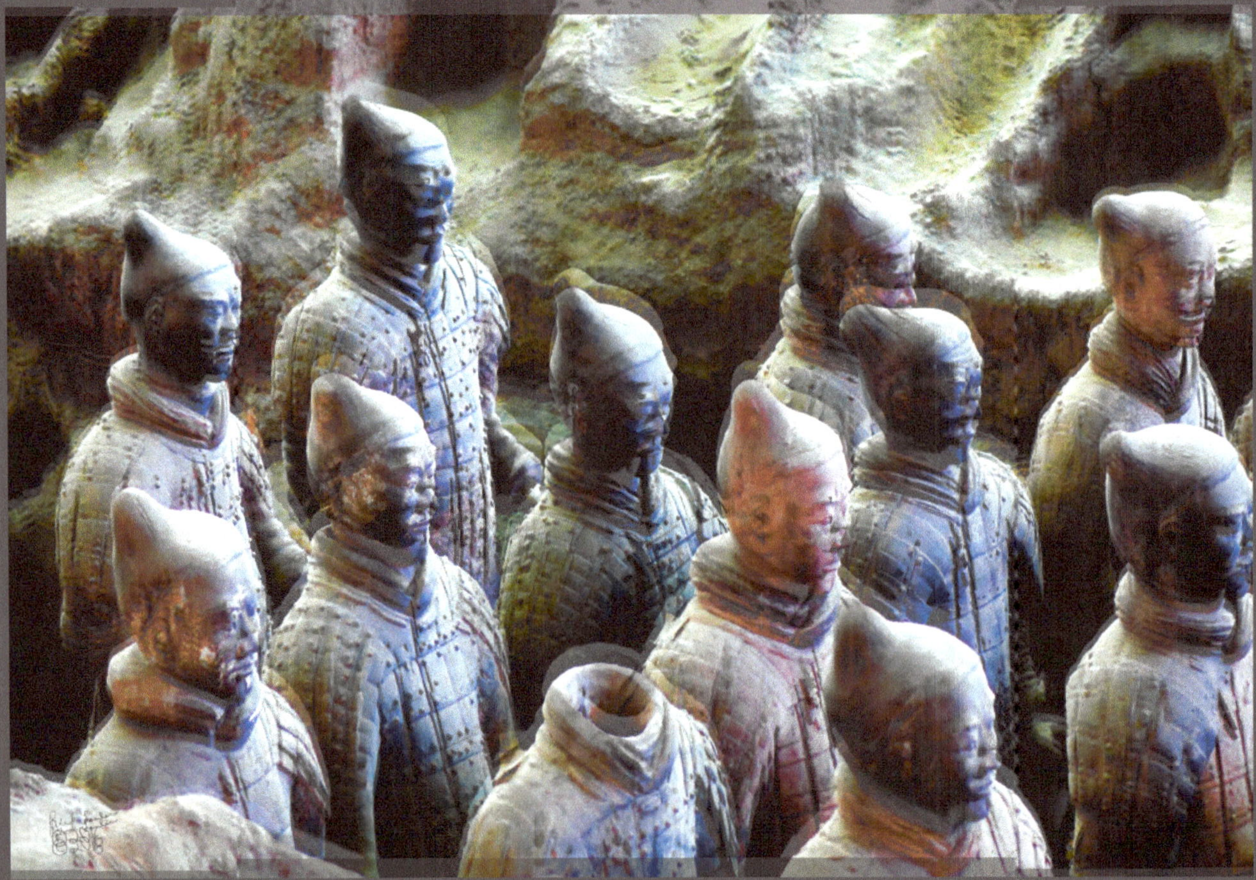

Terracotta Warriors Xi'an

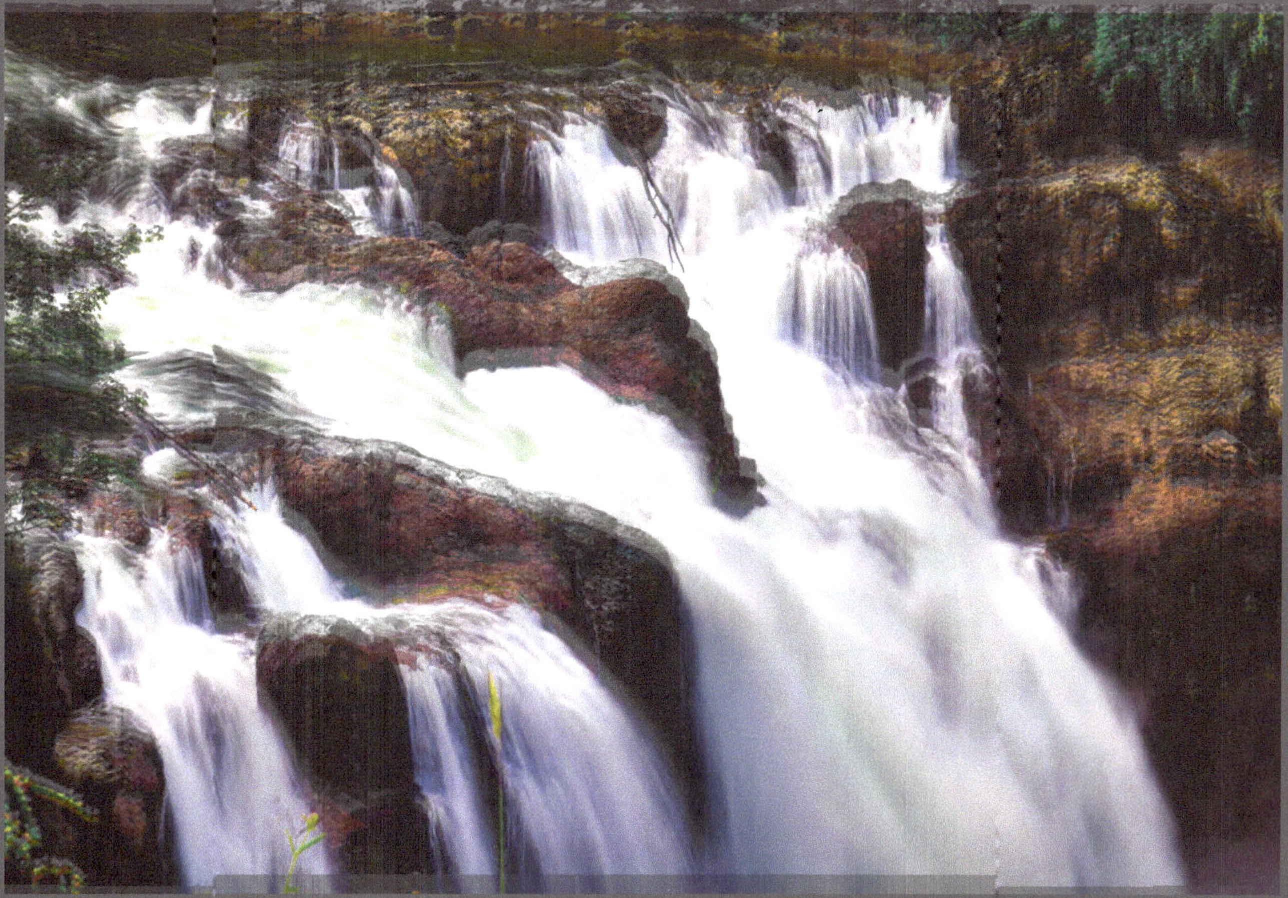

Snoqualmie Falls

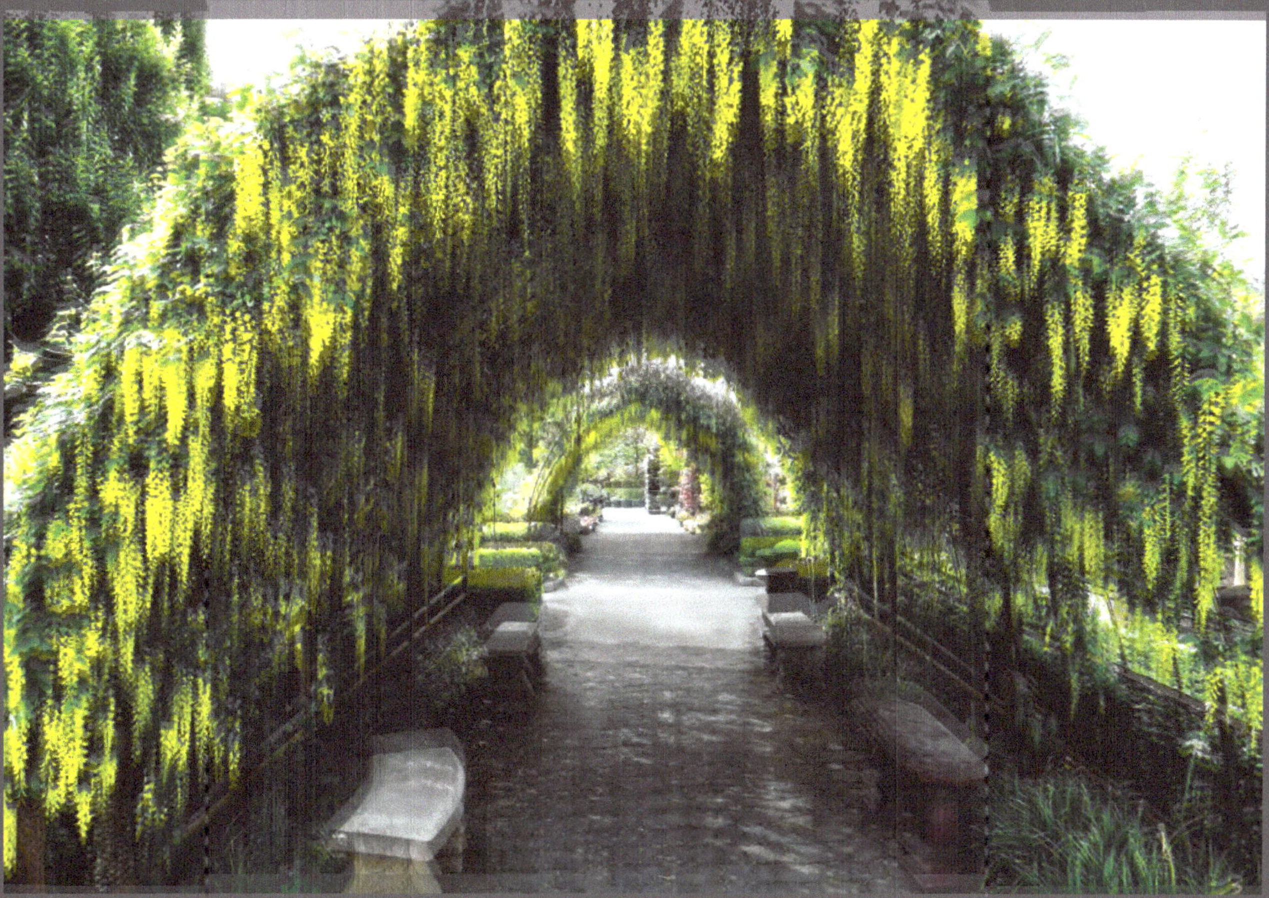

Spring Arbor

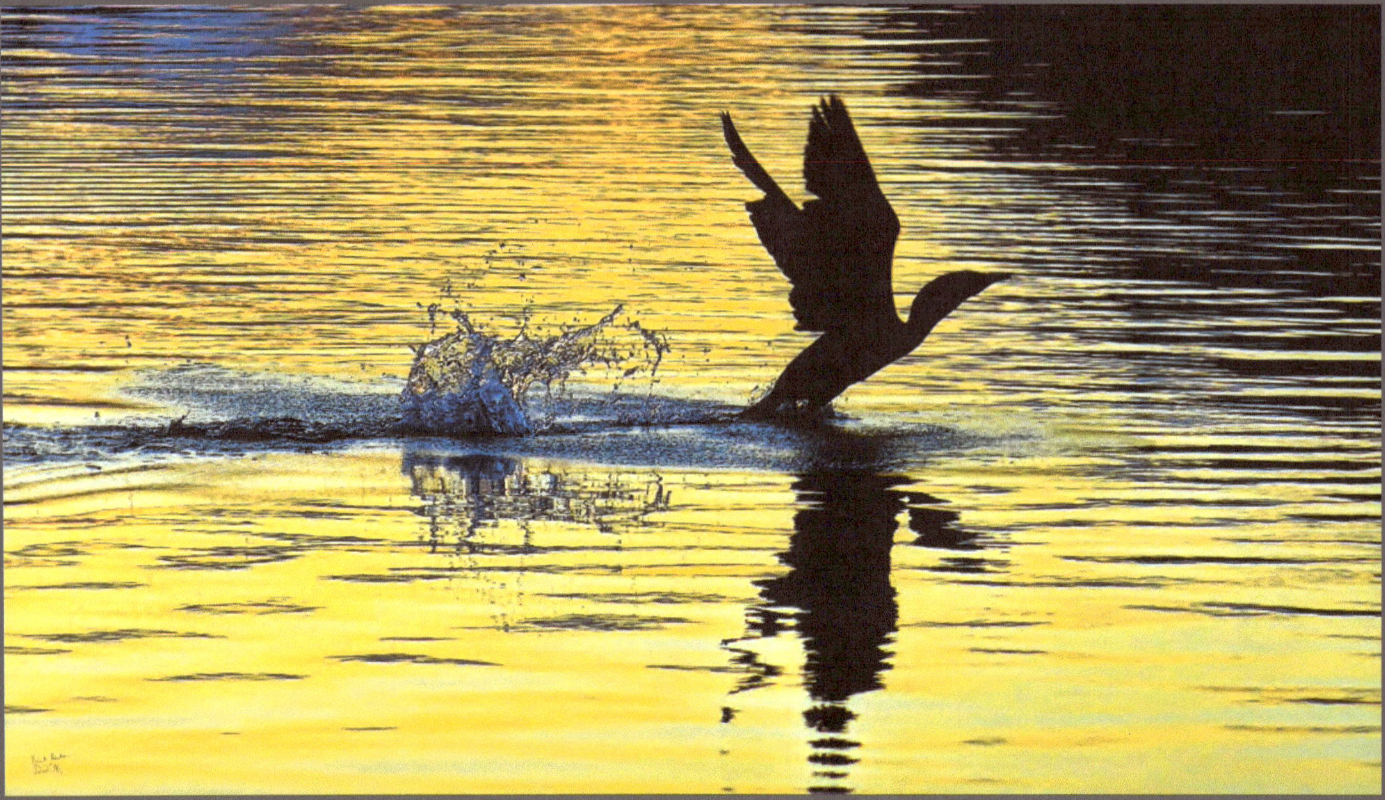

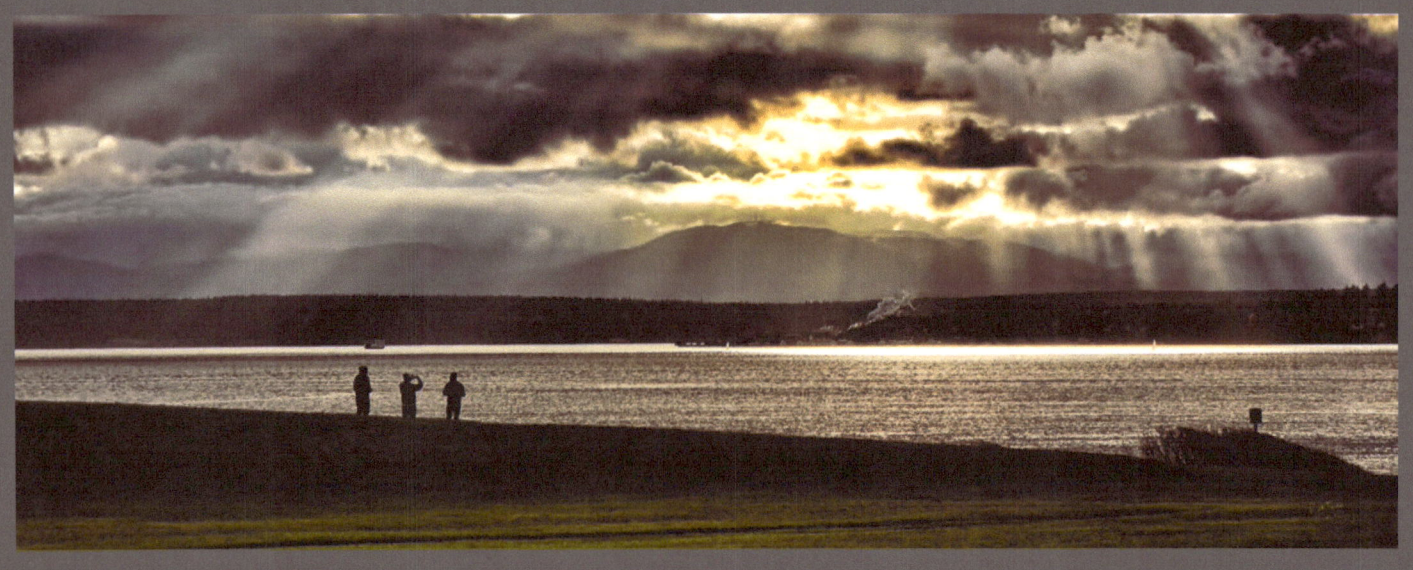

Taking Flight

Raining Sumbeams

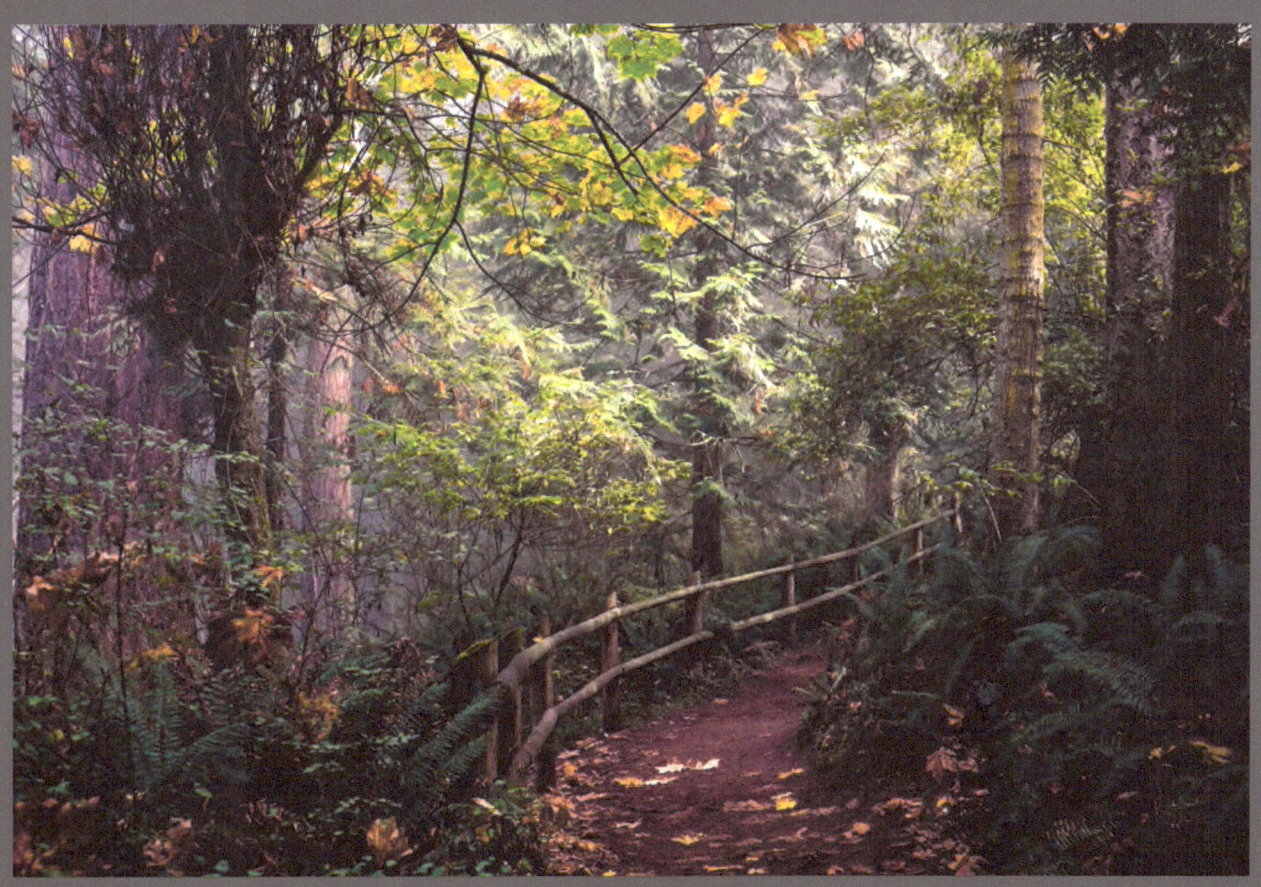

Deception Pass Trail

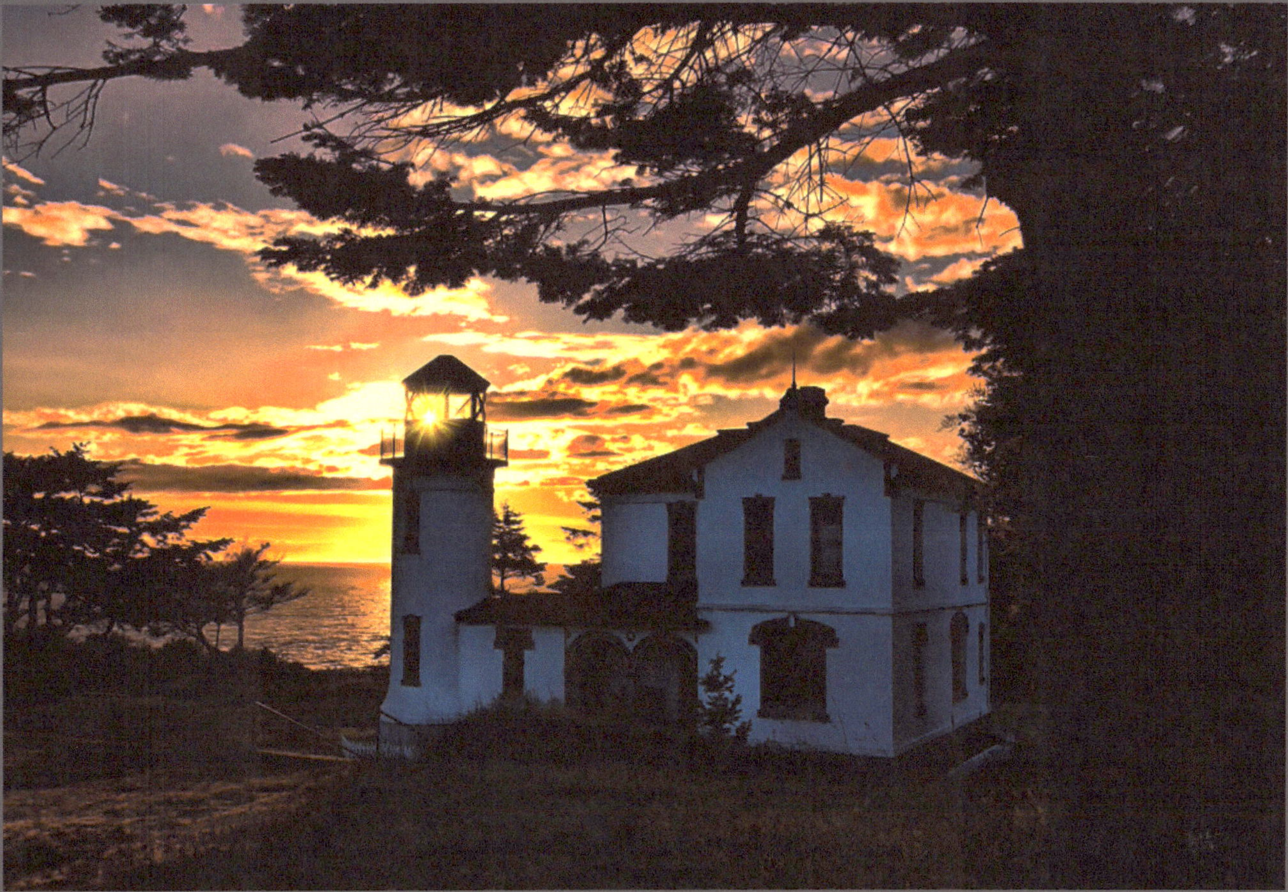

Admiralty Head Lighthouse

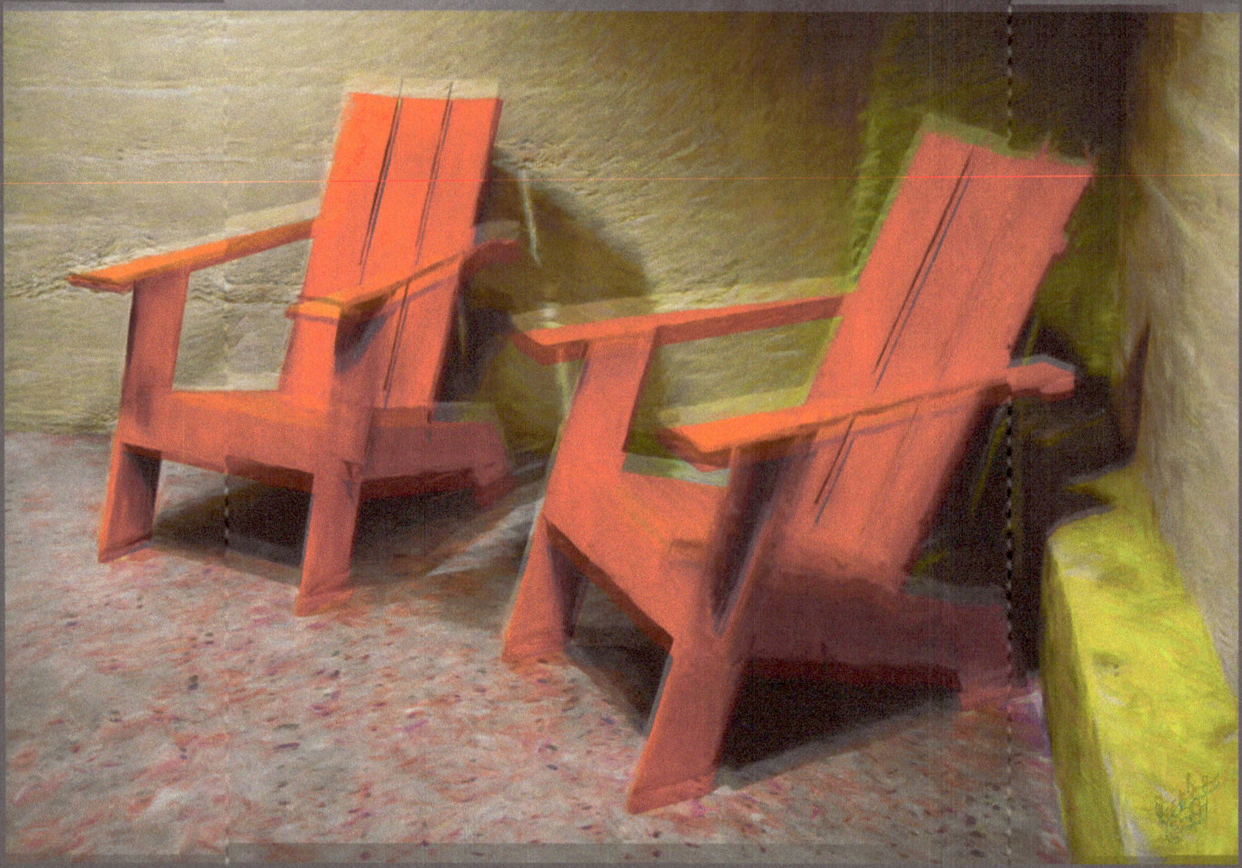

The Red Chairs

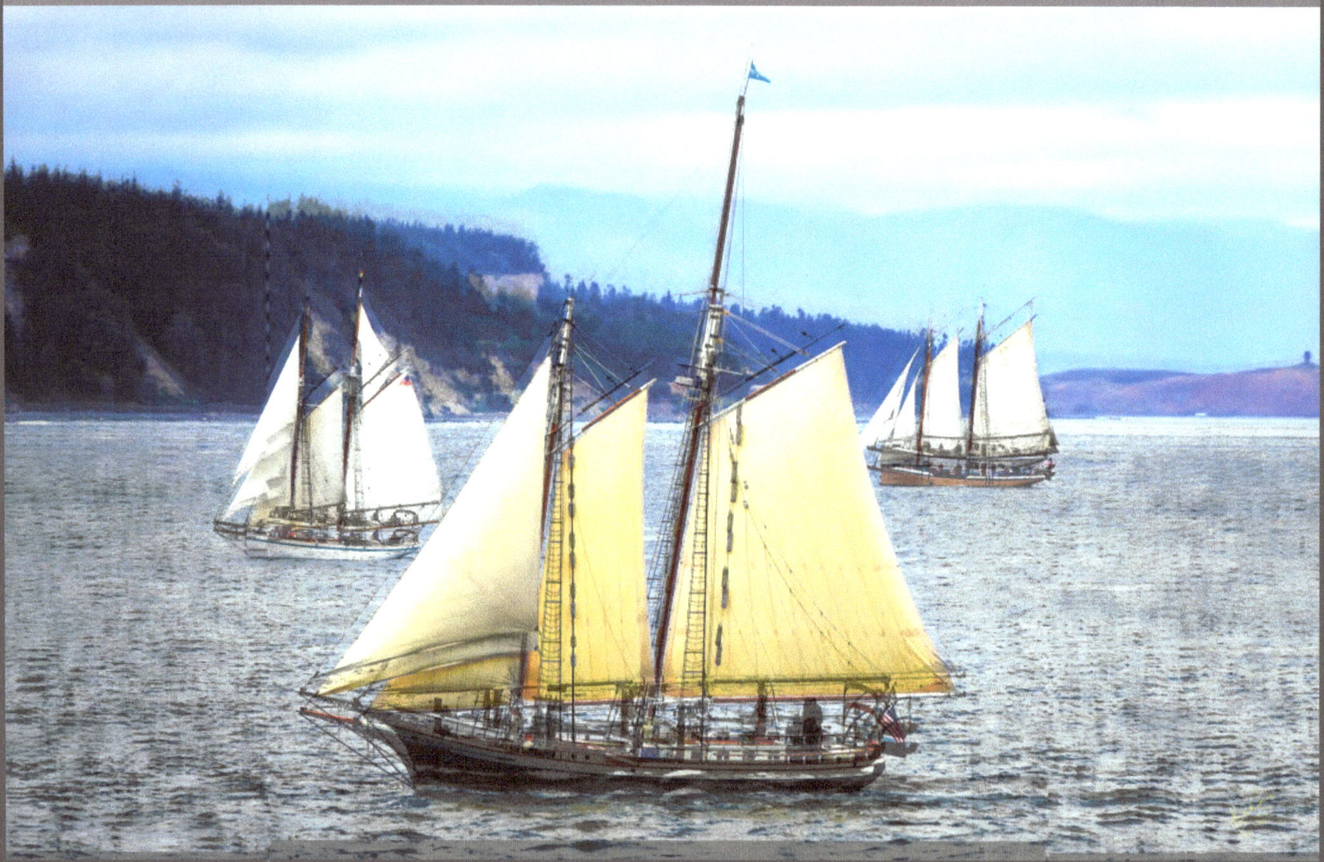

Juan de Fuca Flotilla

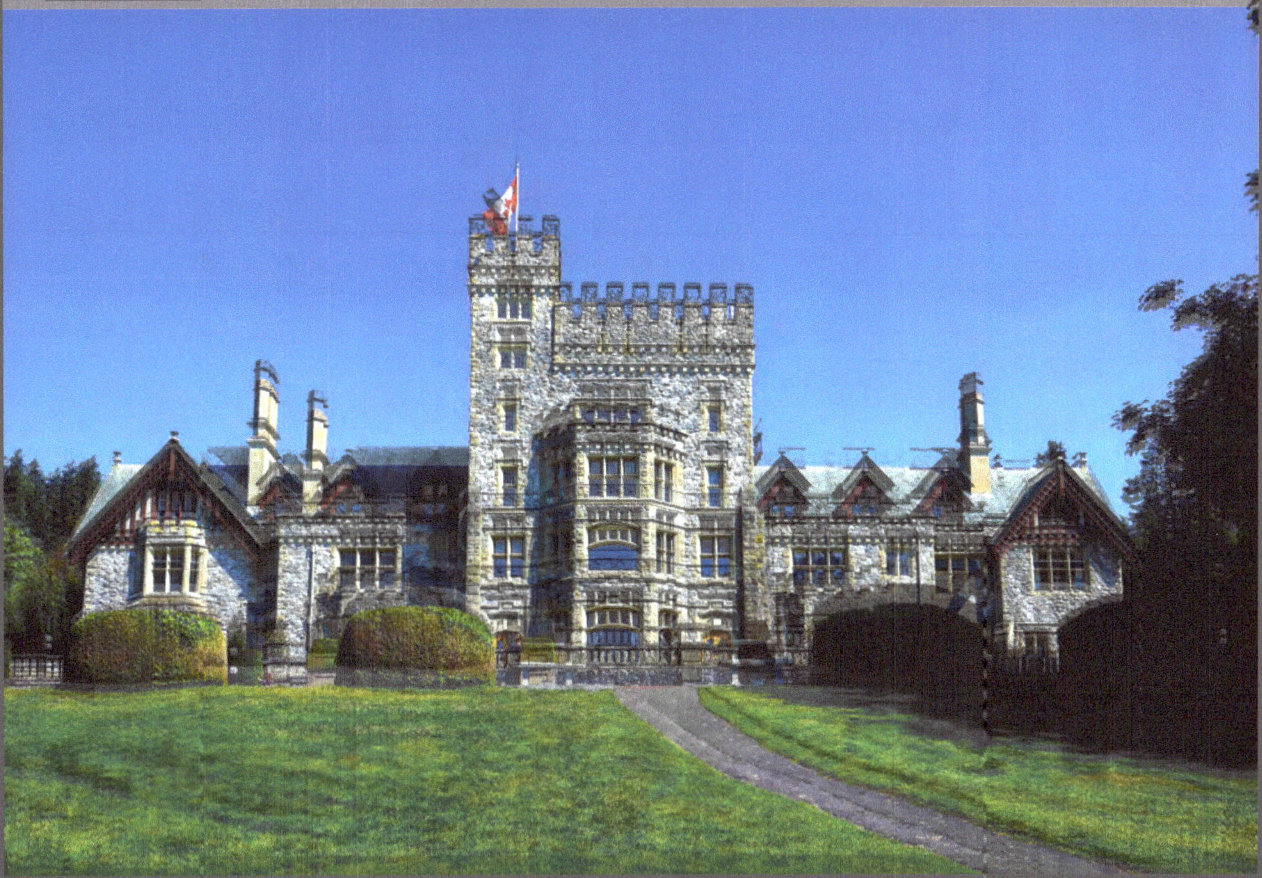

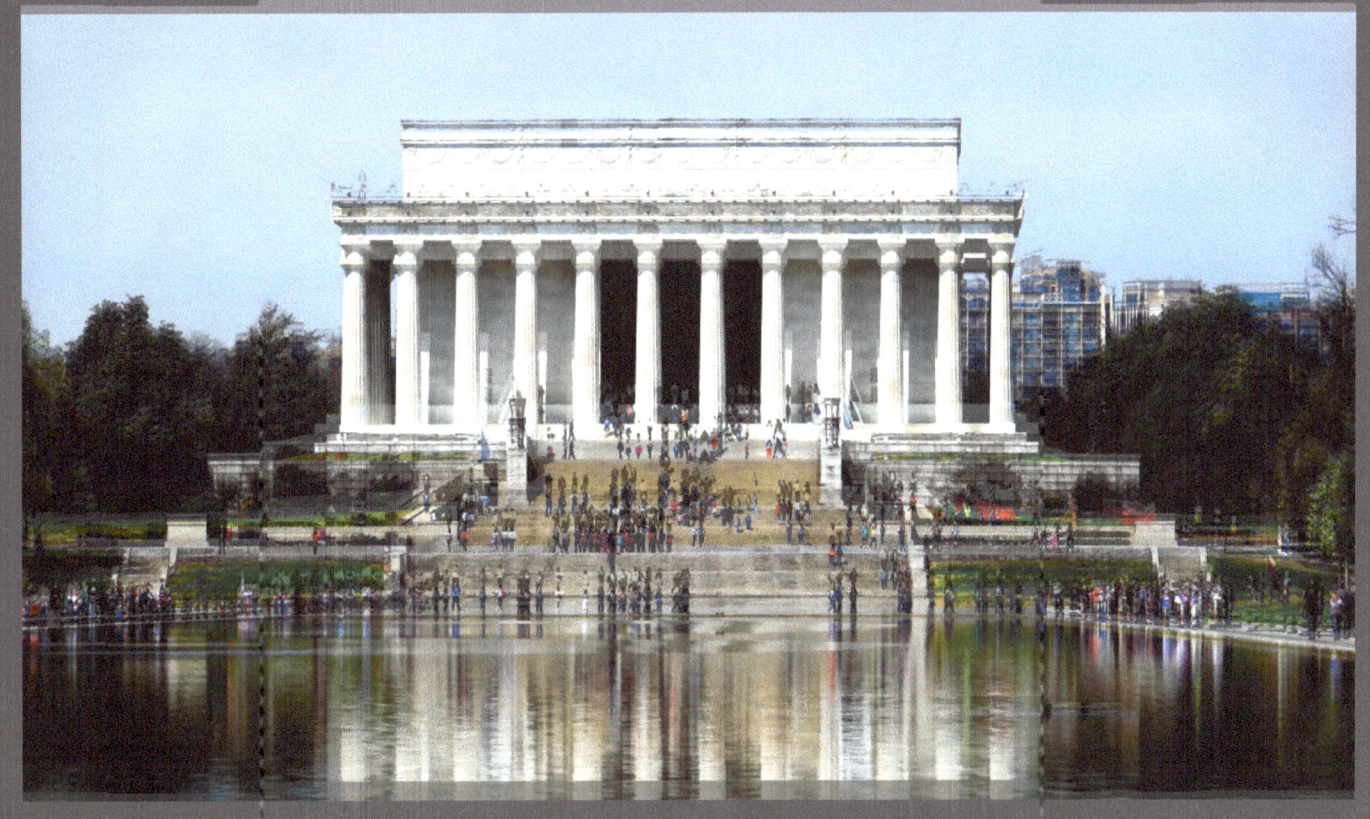

School for Mutants

Memorial

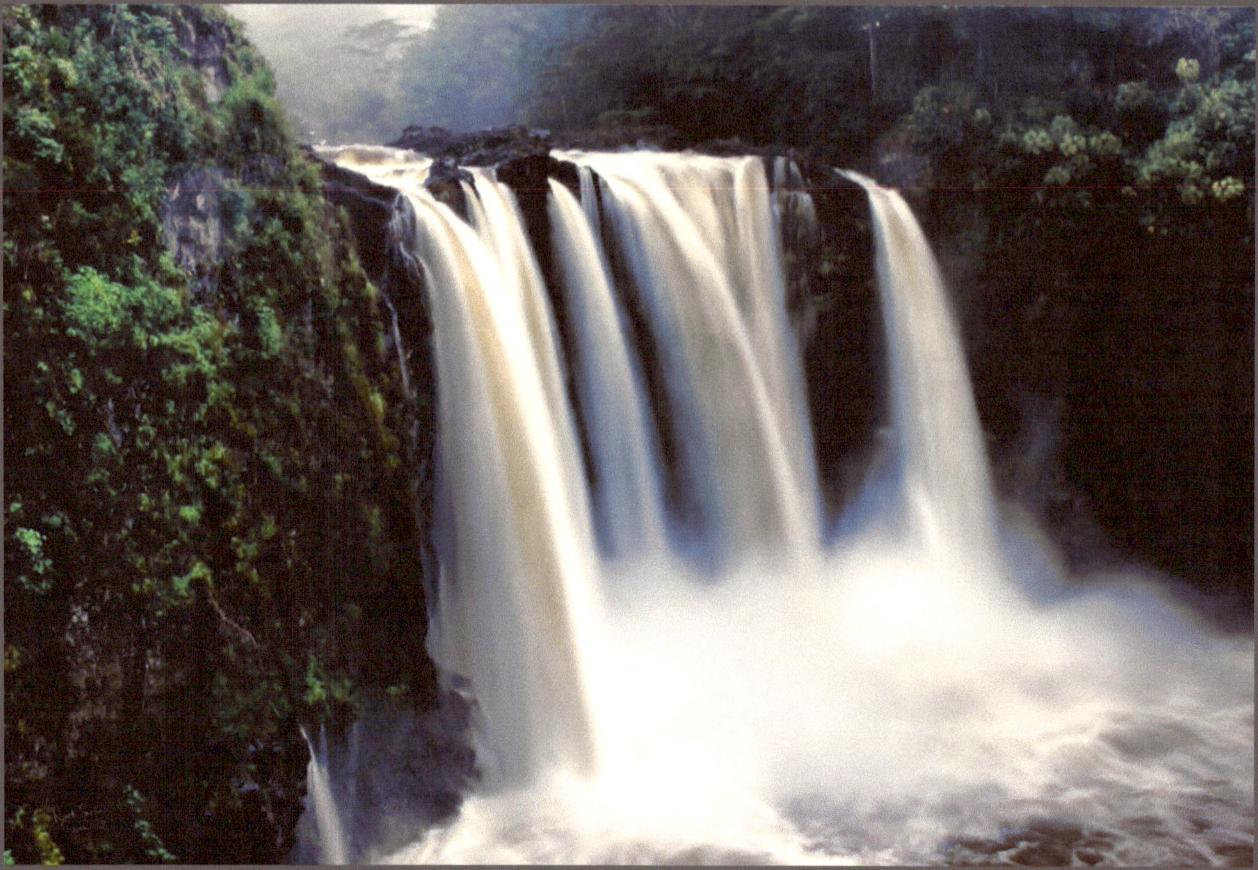

Rainbow Falls

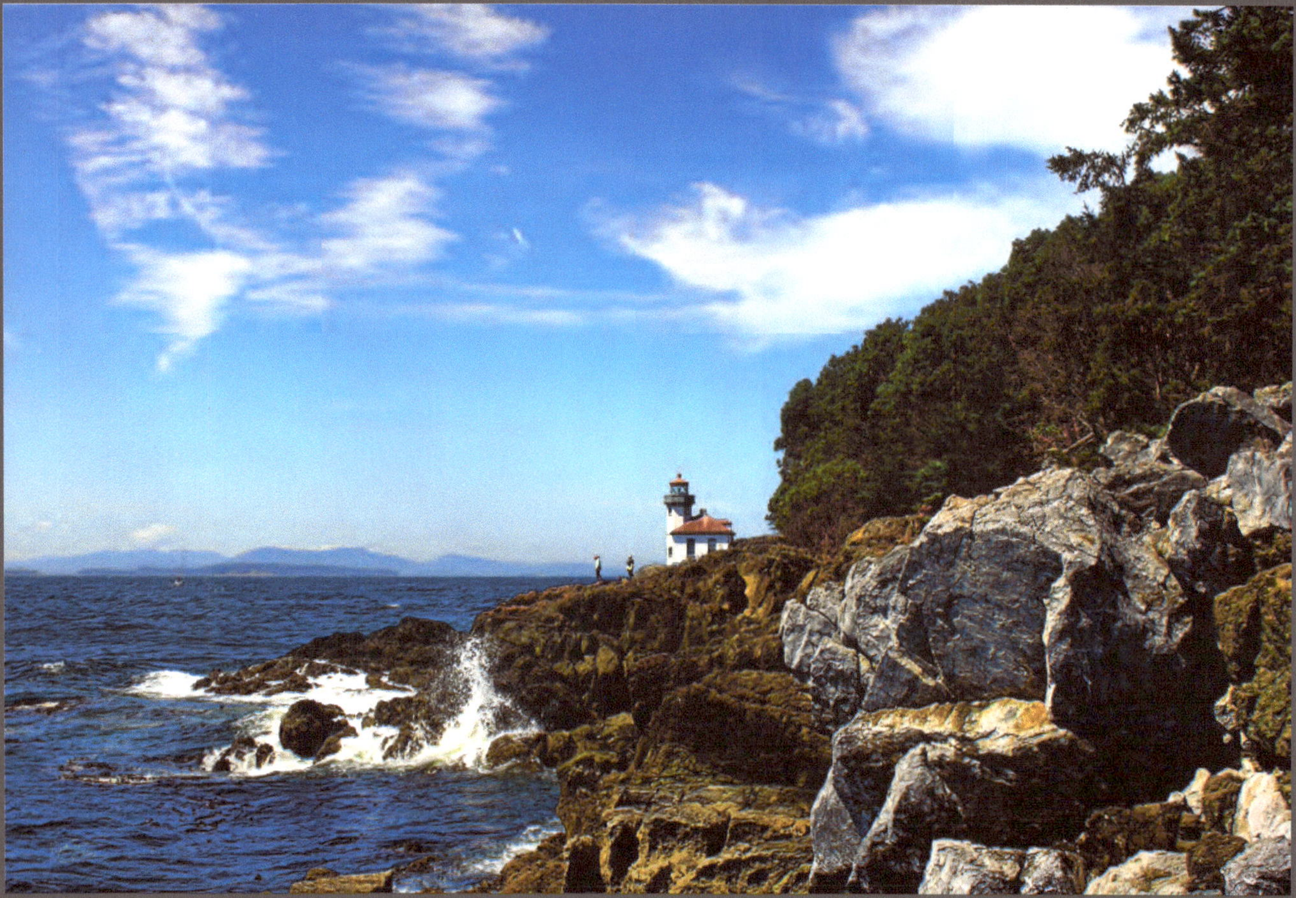

Lime Kiln Lighthouse

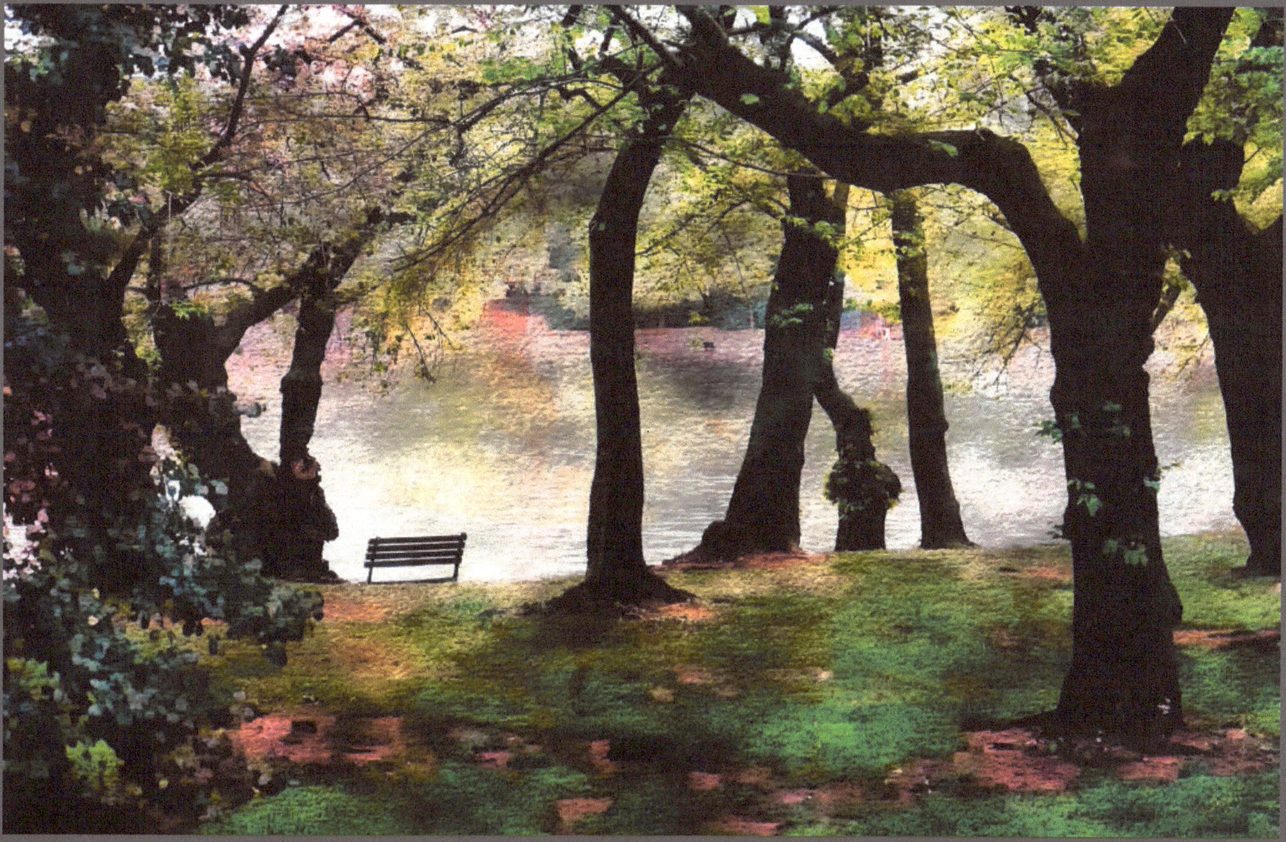

D.C. Rendezvous

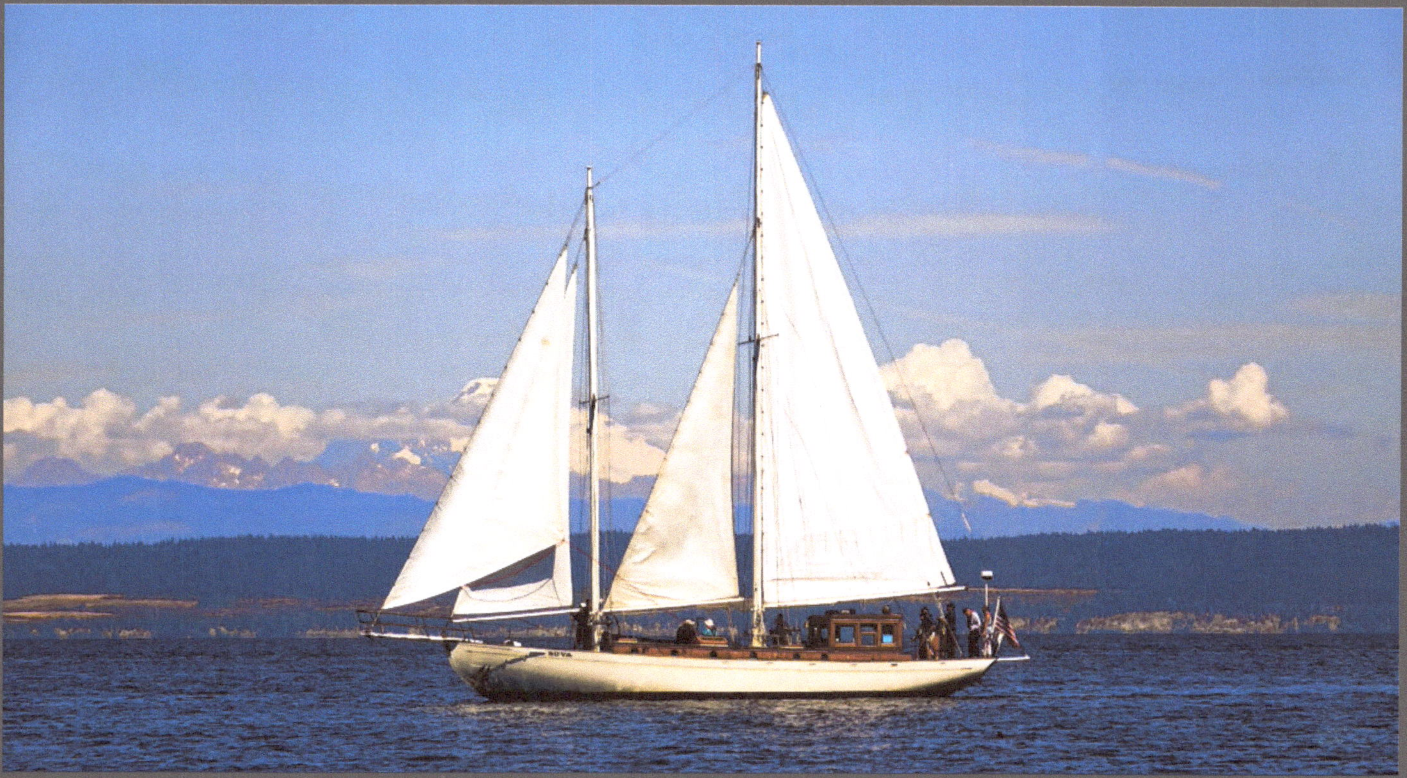

Suva Sailing

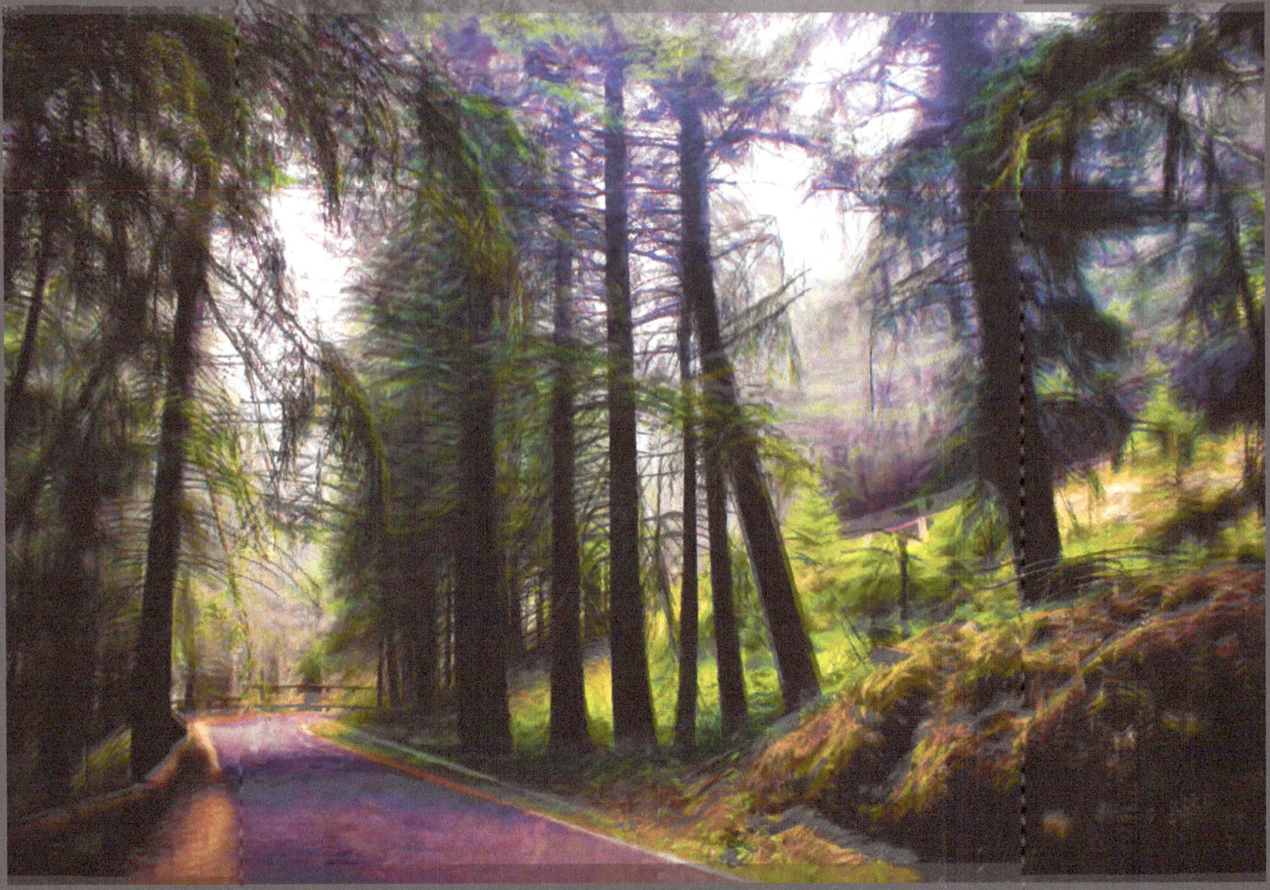

Mt. Constitution

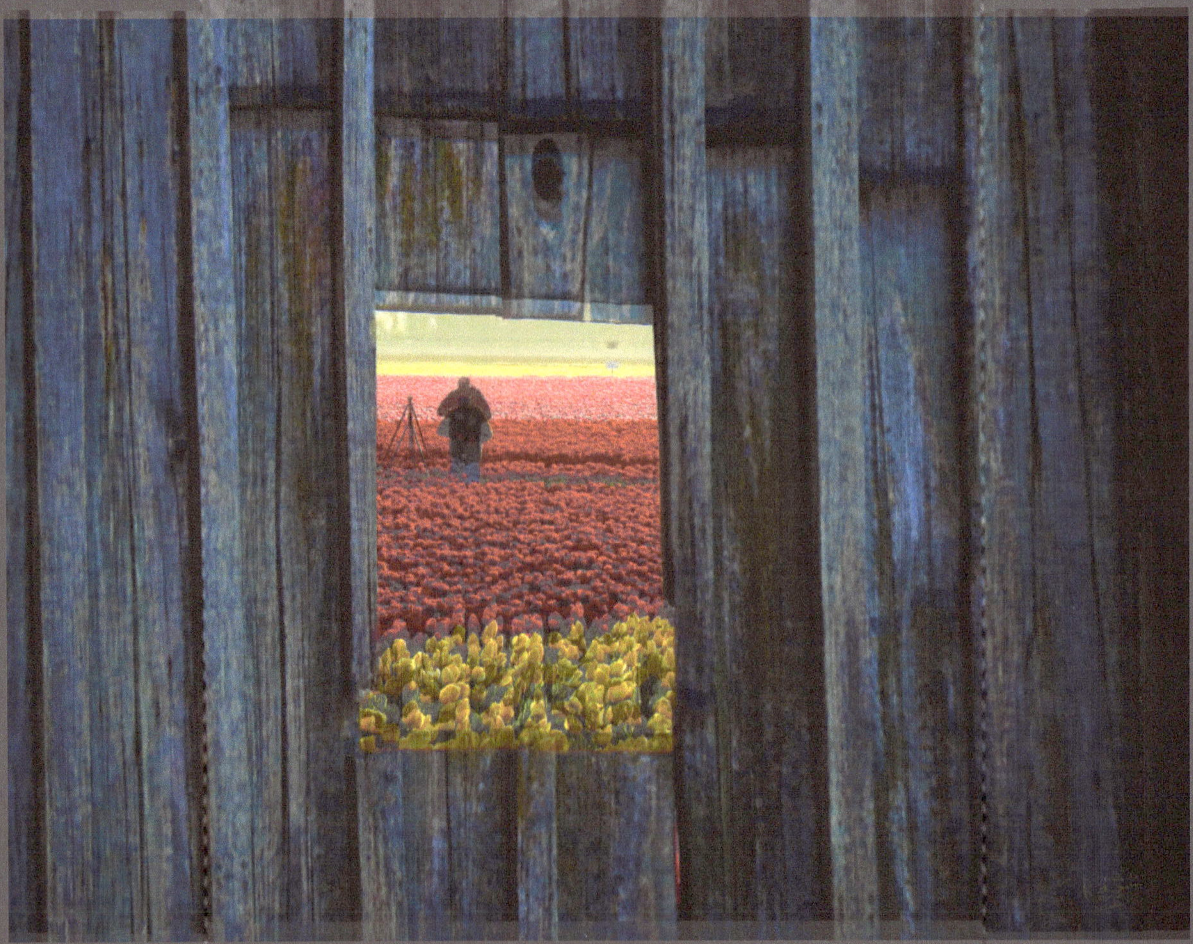

The Window

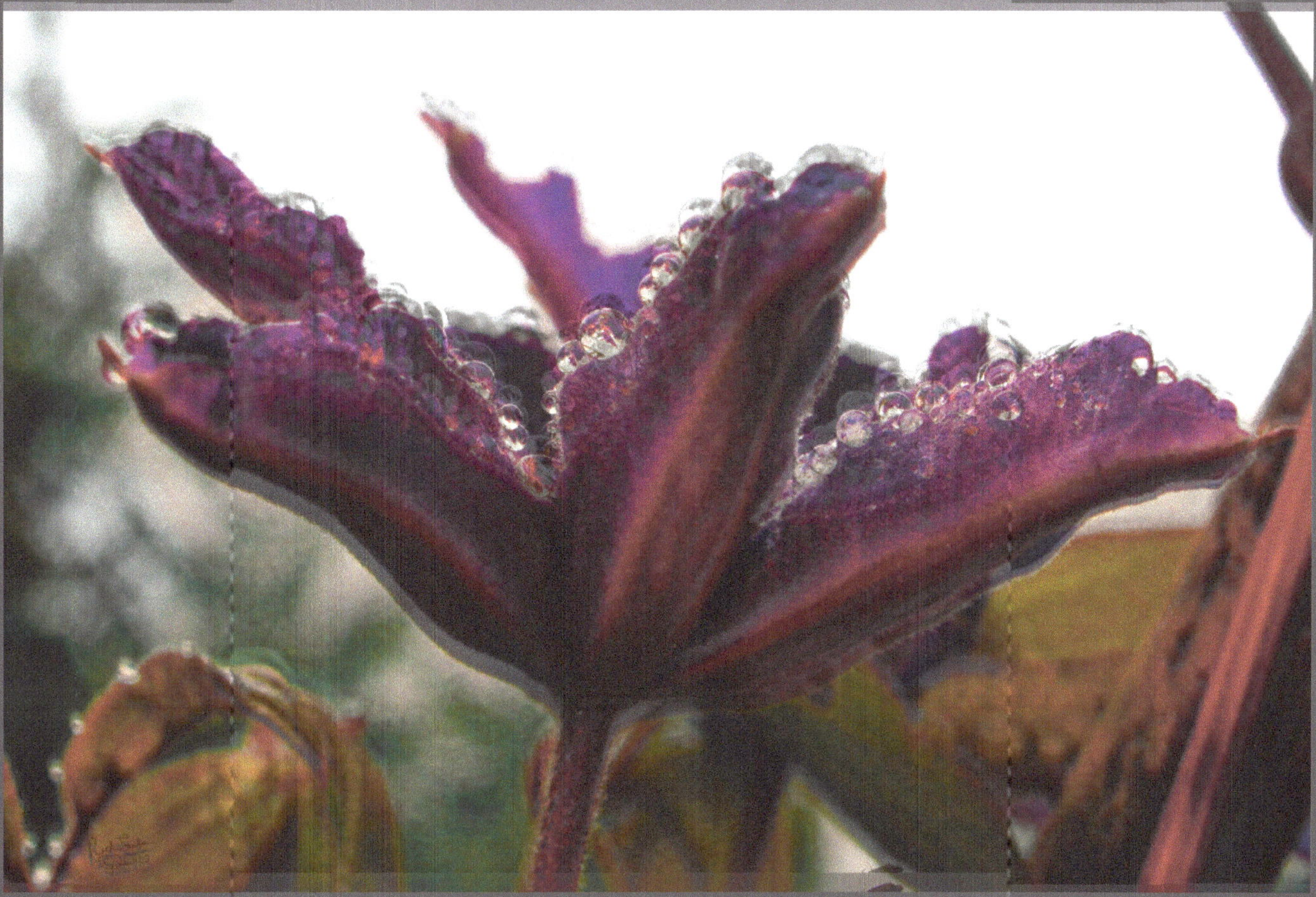

Raindrops on Petals

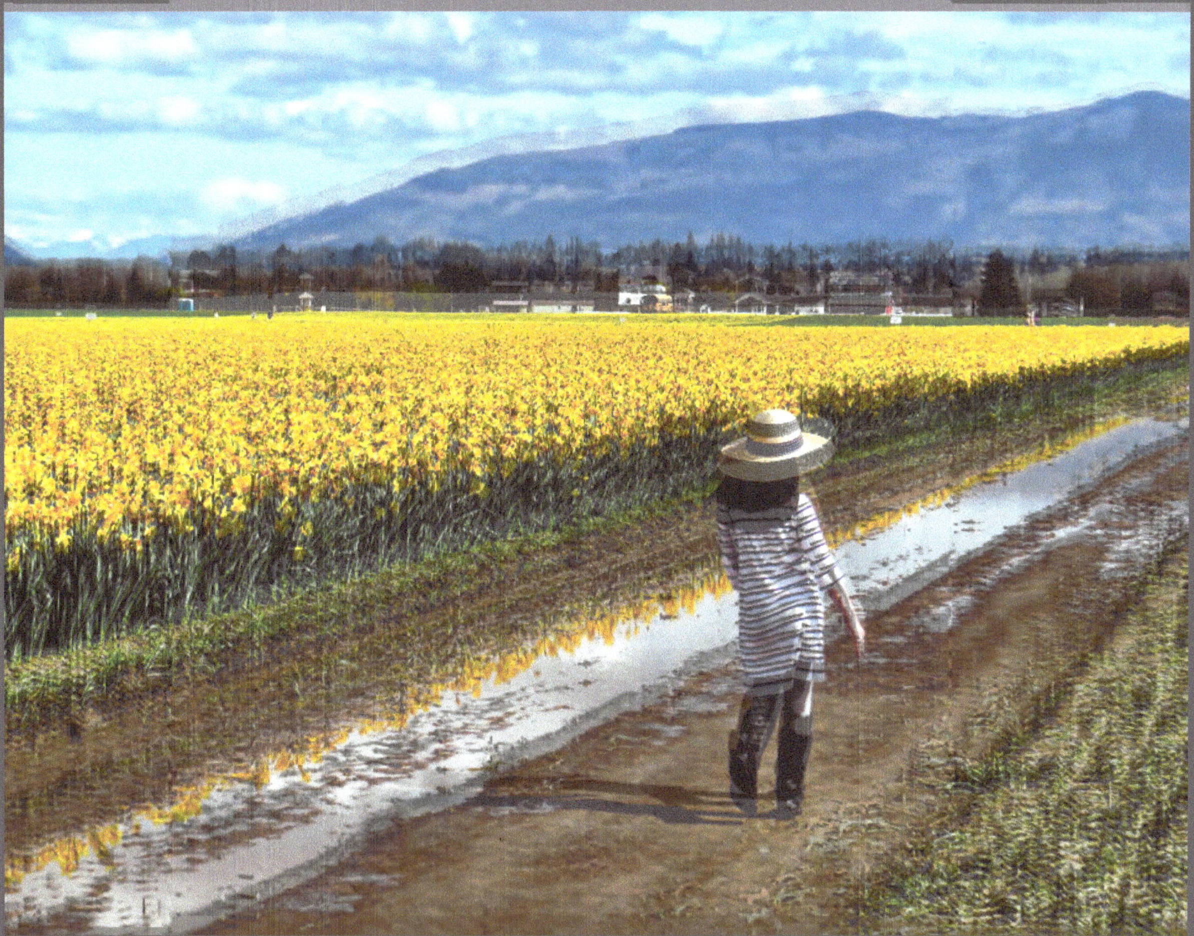

Dancing the Daffodils

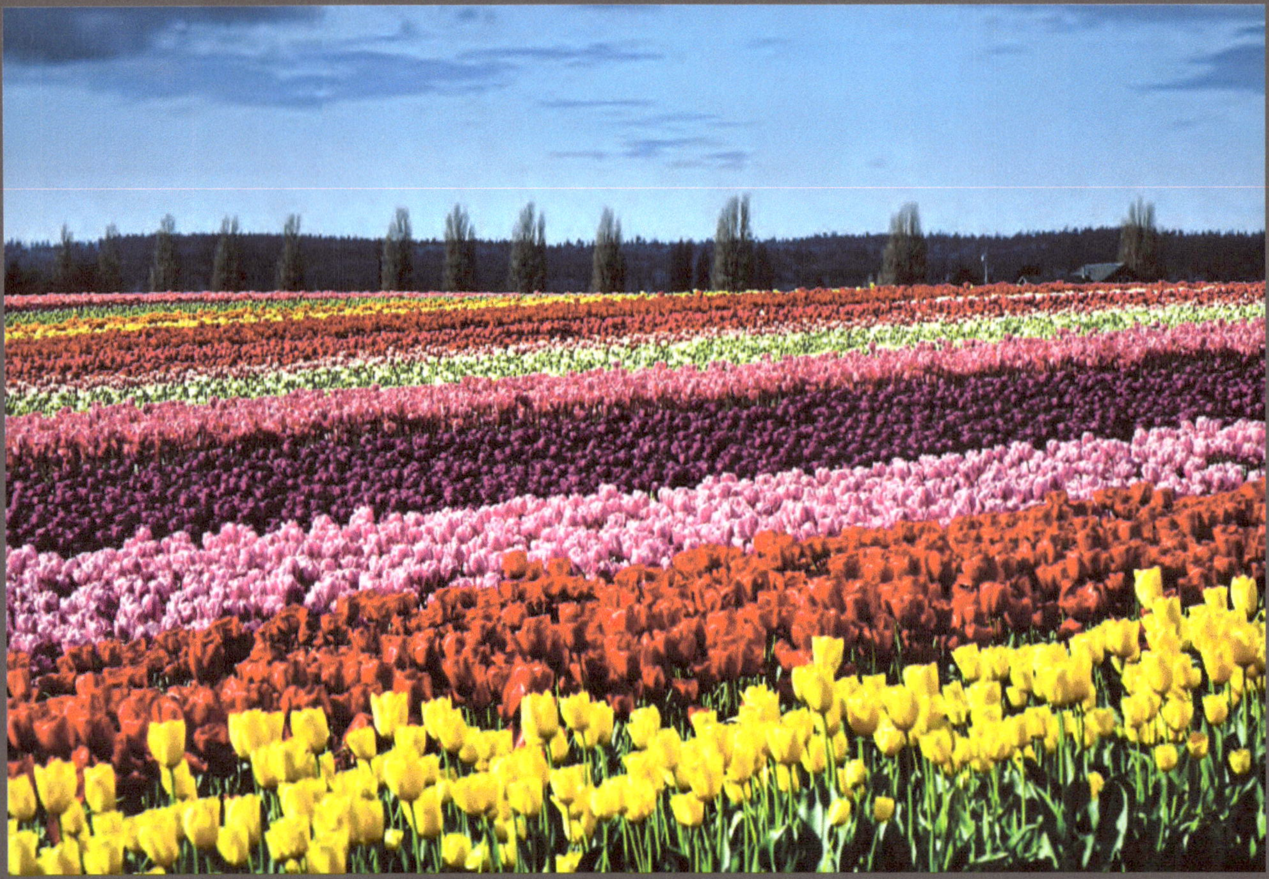

Tulip Field

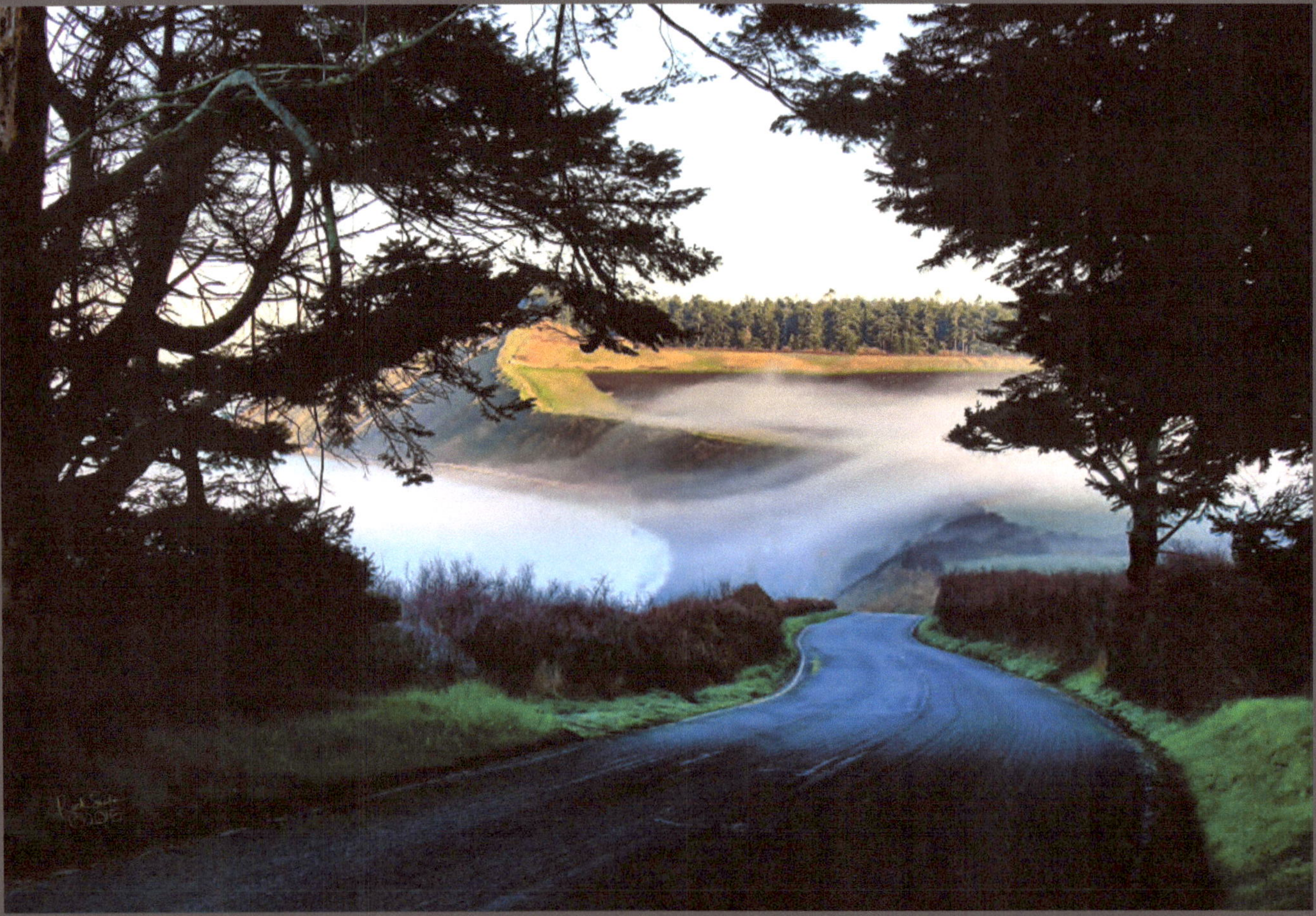

Fog on the Prairie

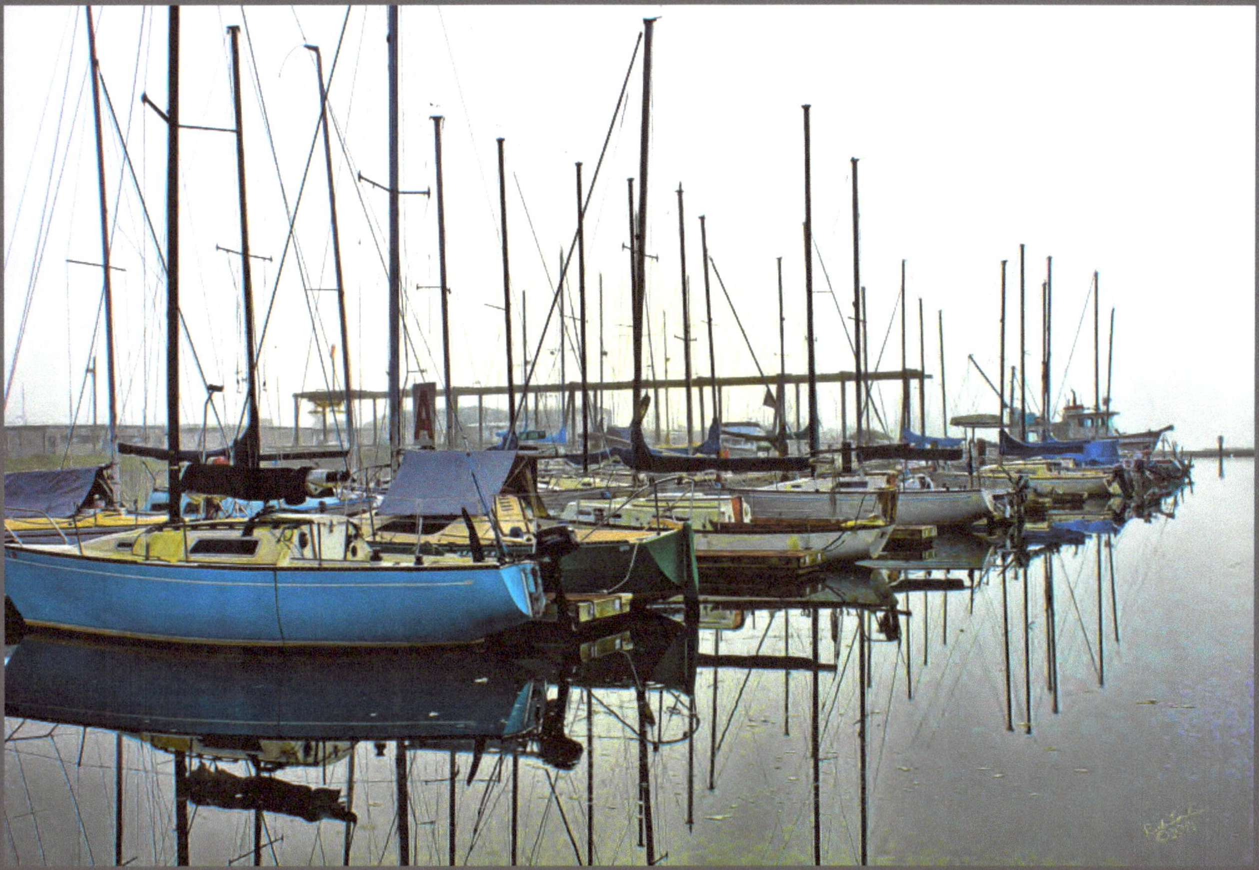

Calm on the Marina

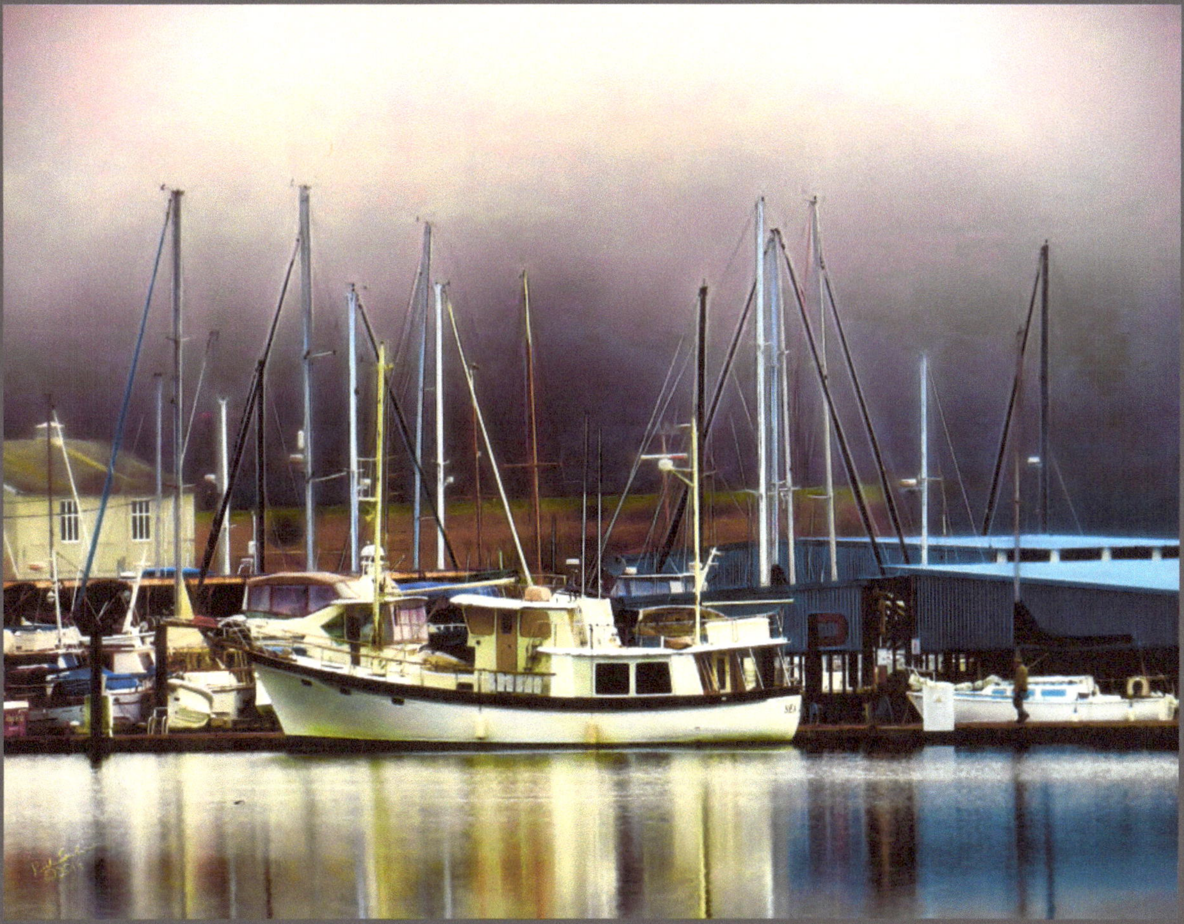

Fog in the Morning

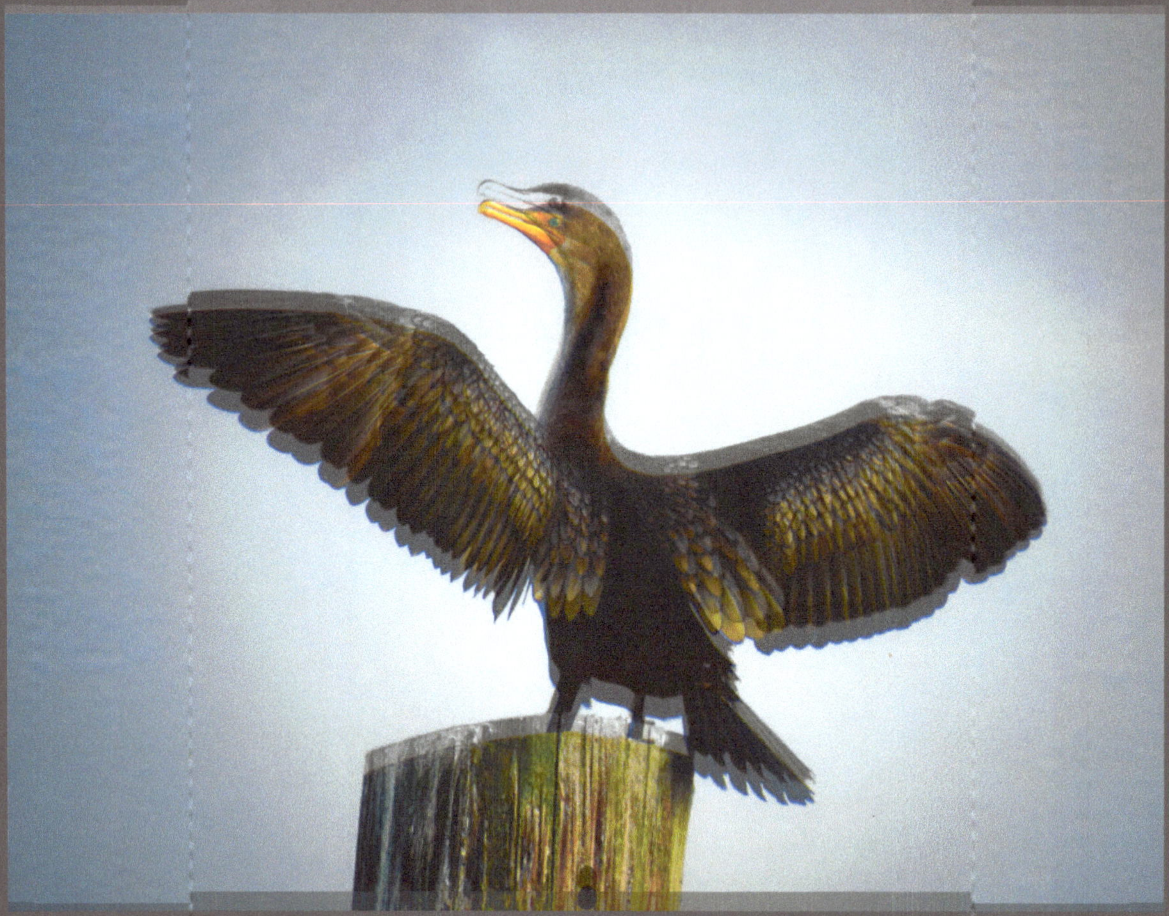

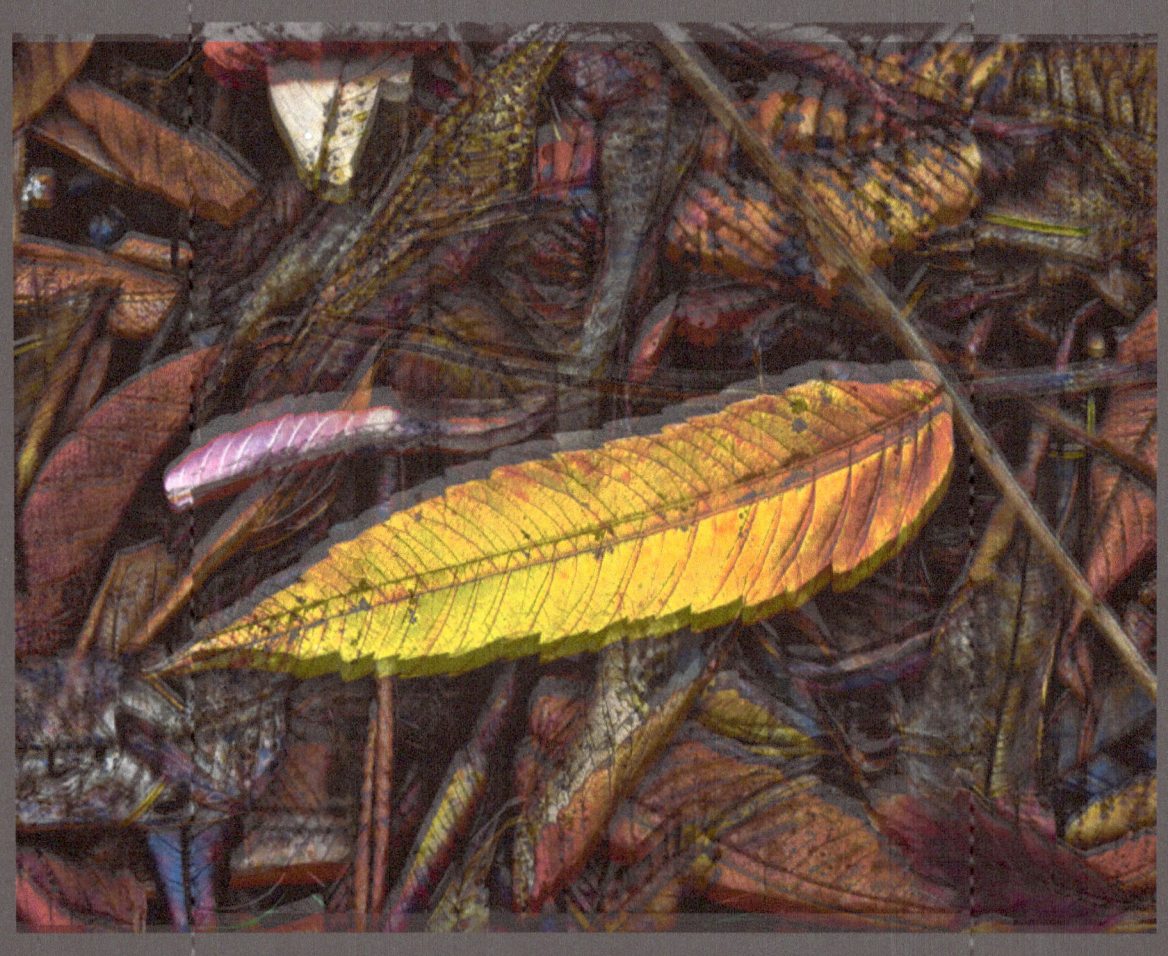

Cormorant Pose

Season of Leaves

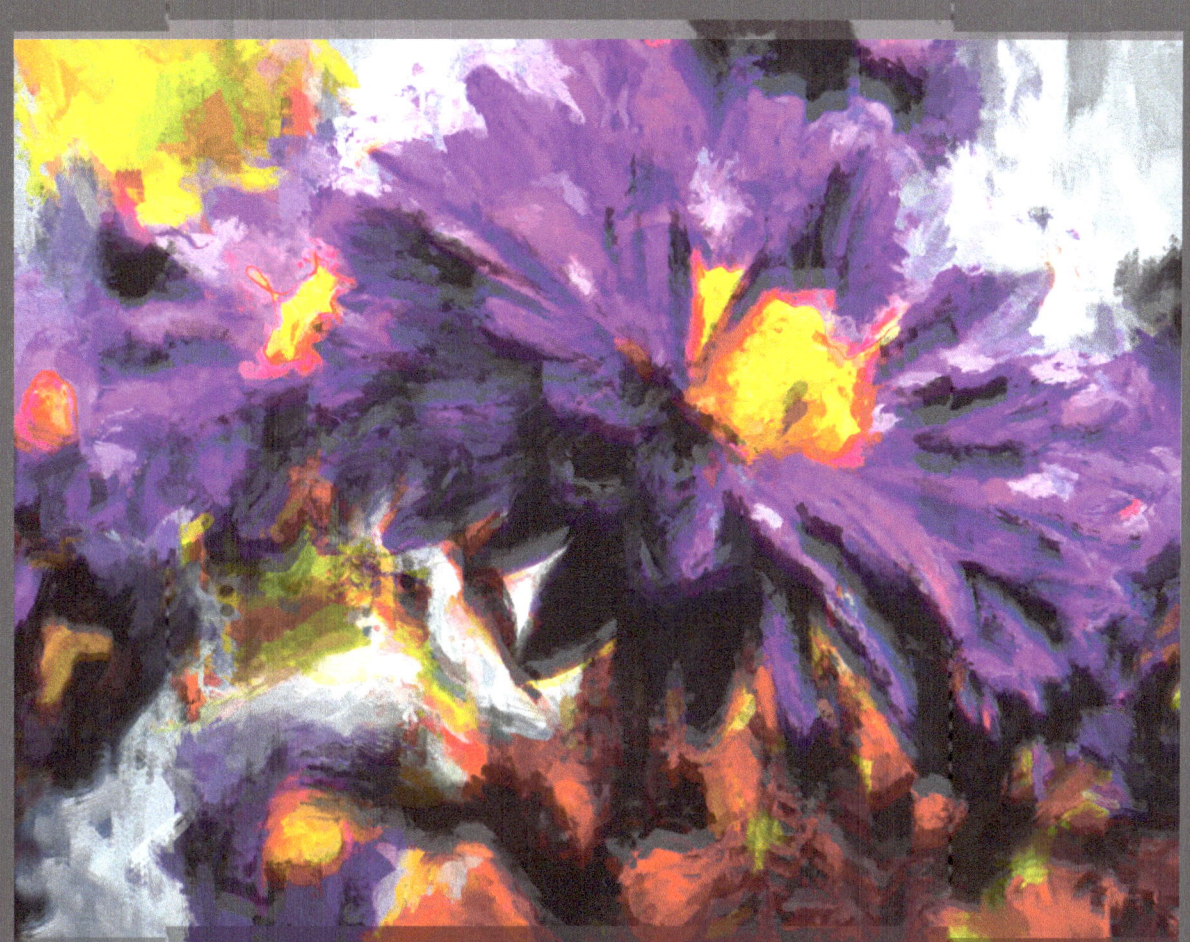

Flowers of my Mind

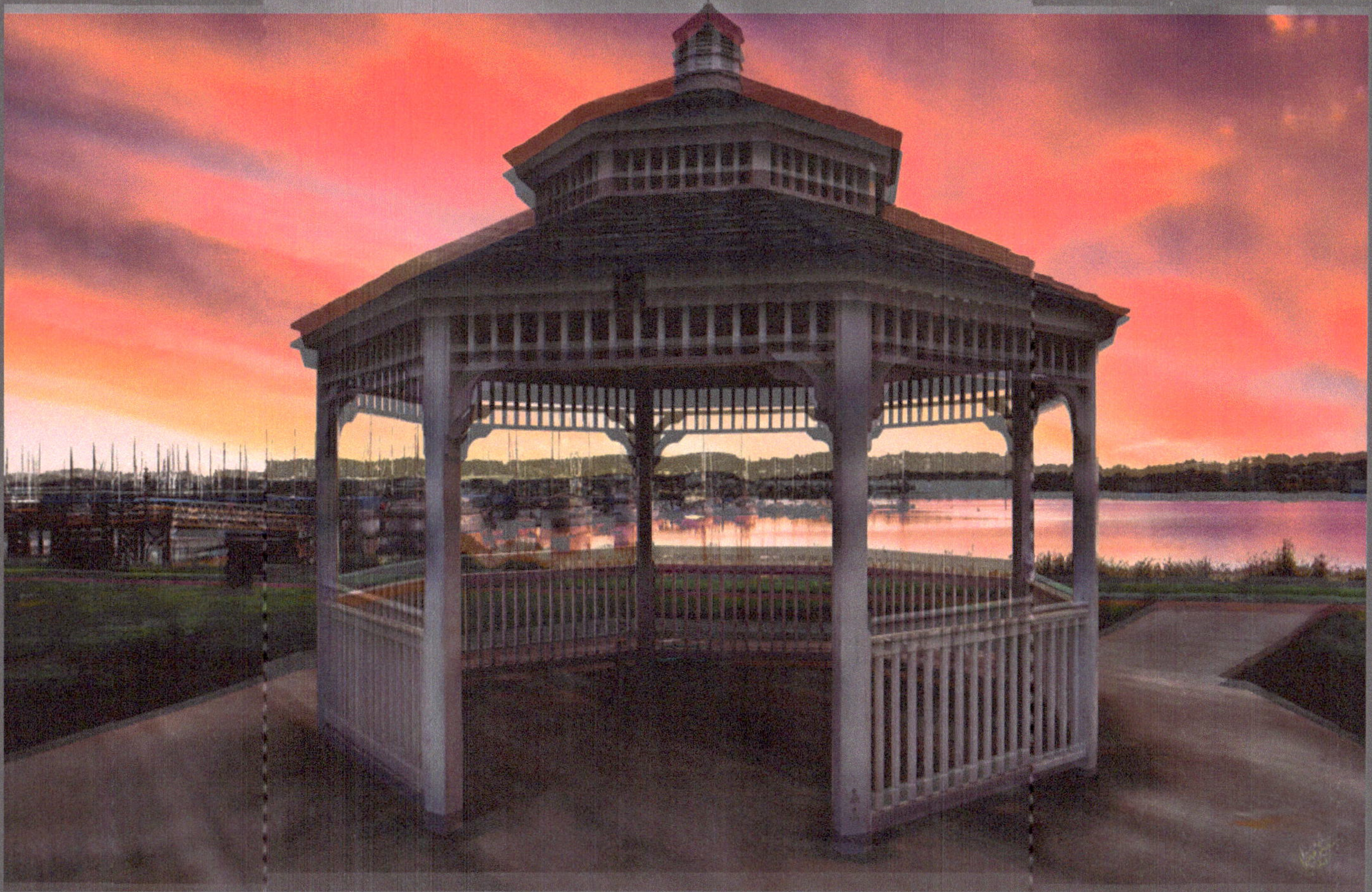

Gazebo Sunset

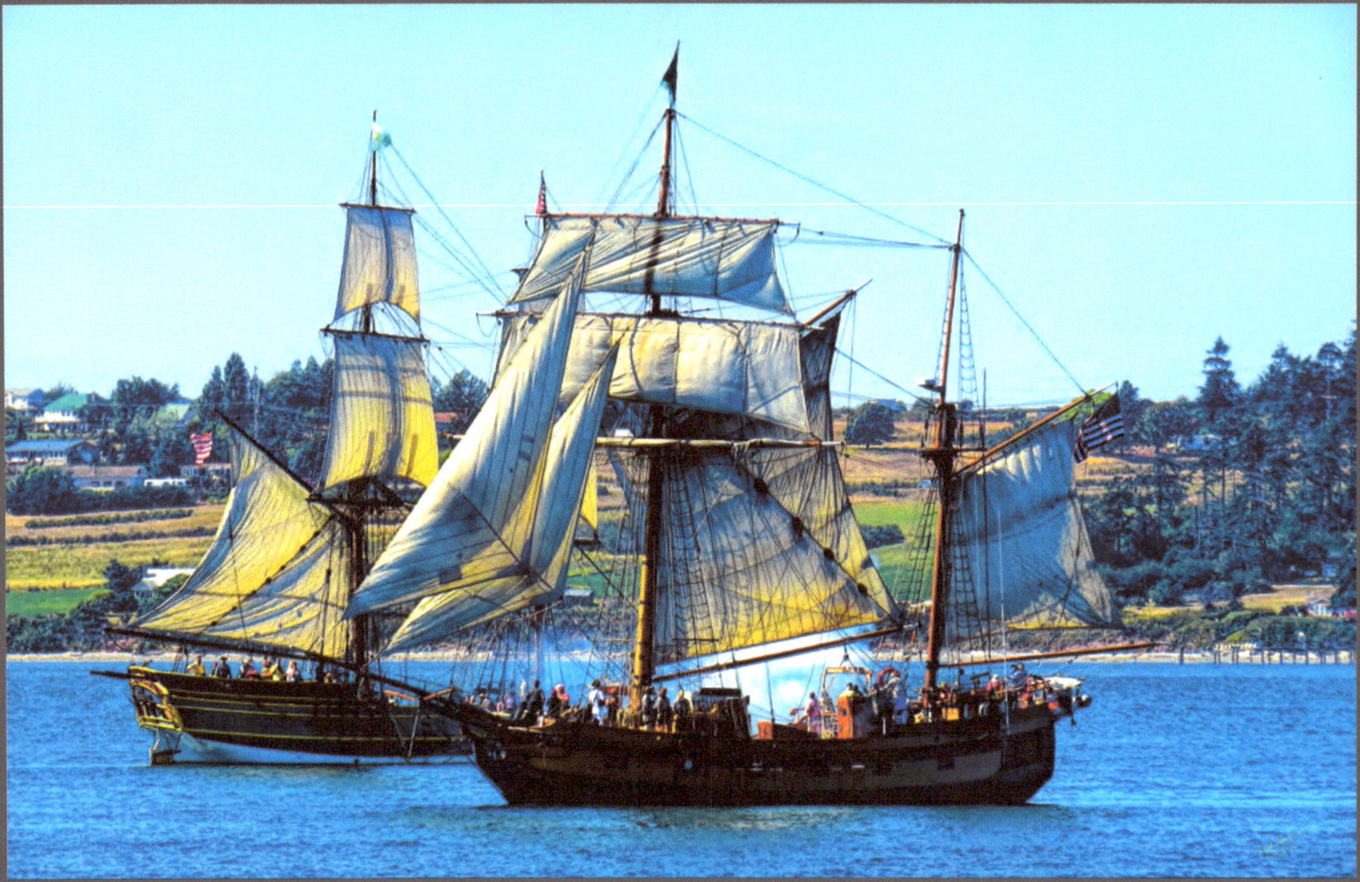

Battle for Penn Cove

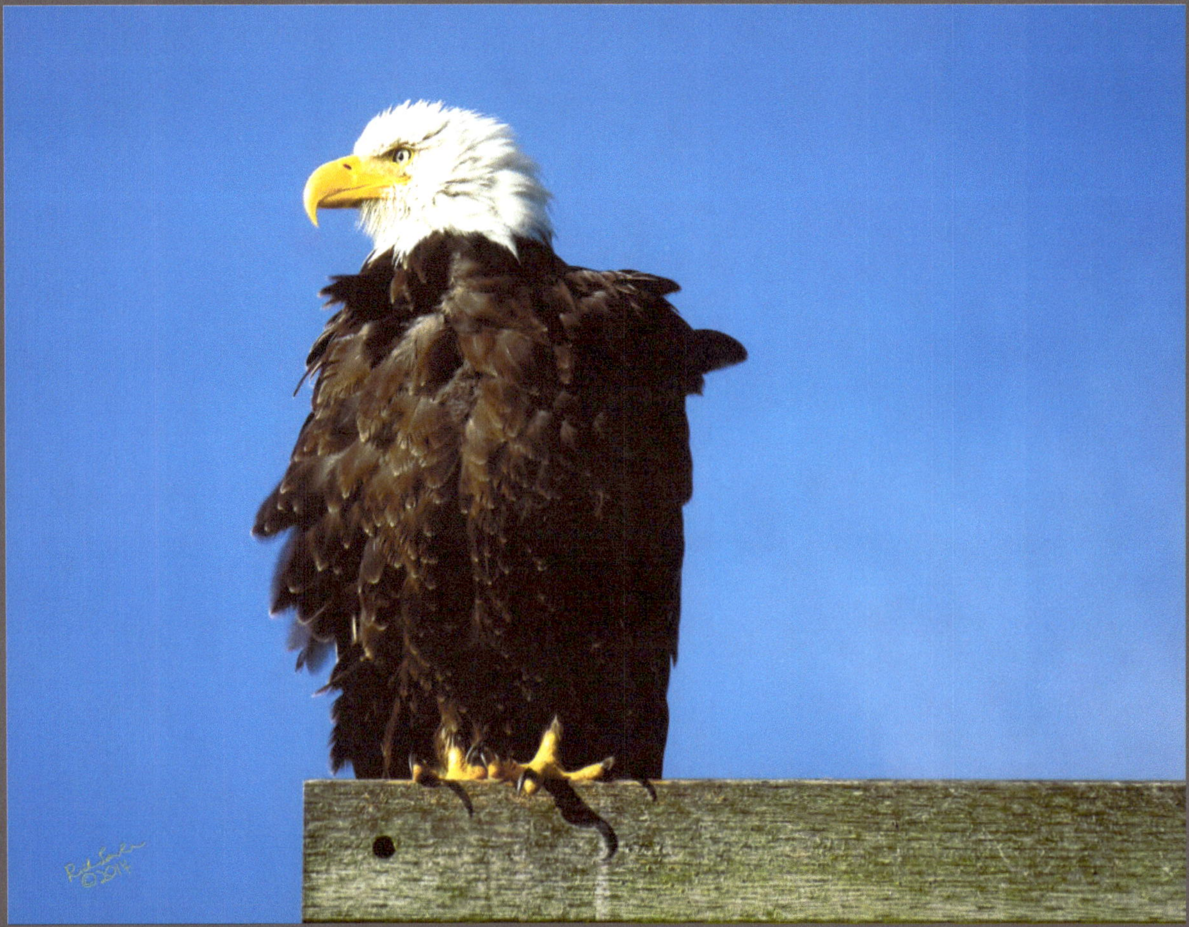

The Eagle Has Landed

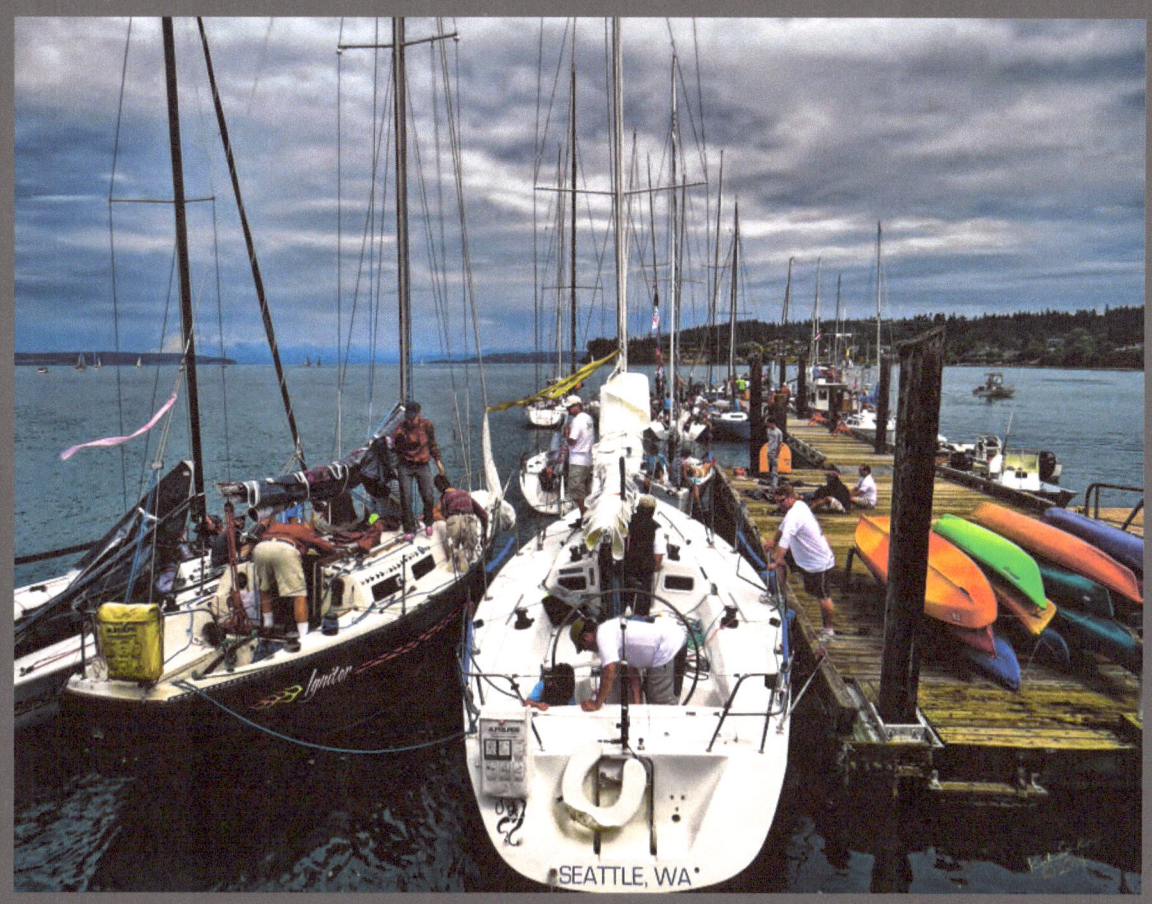

Preparing for the Race

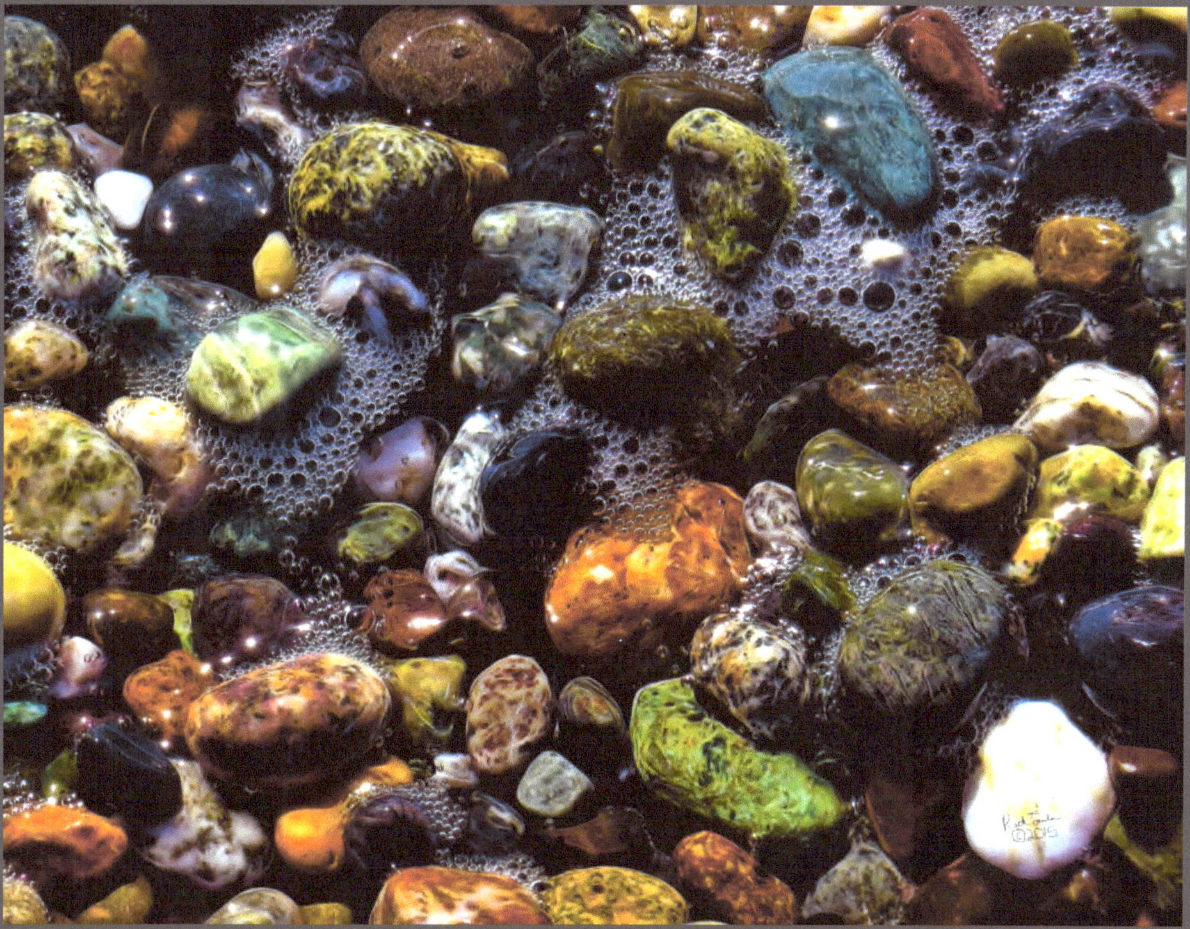

Beach Rocks

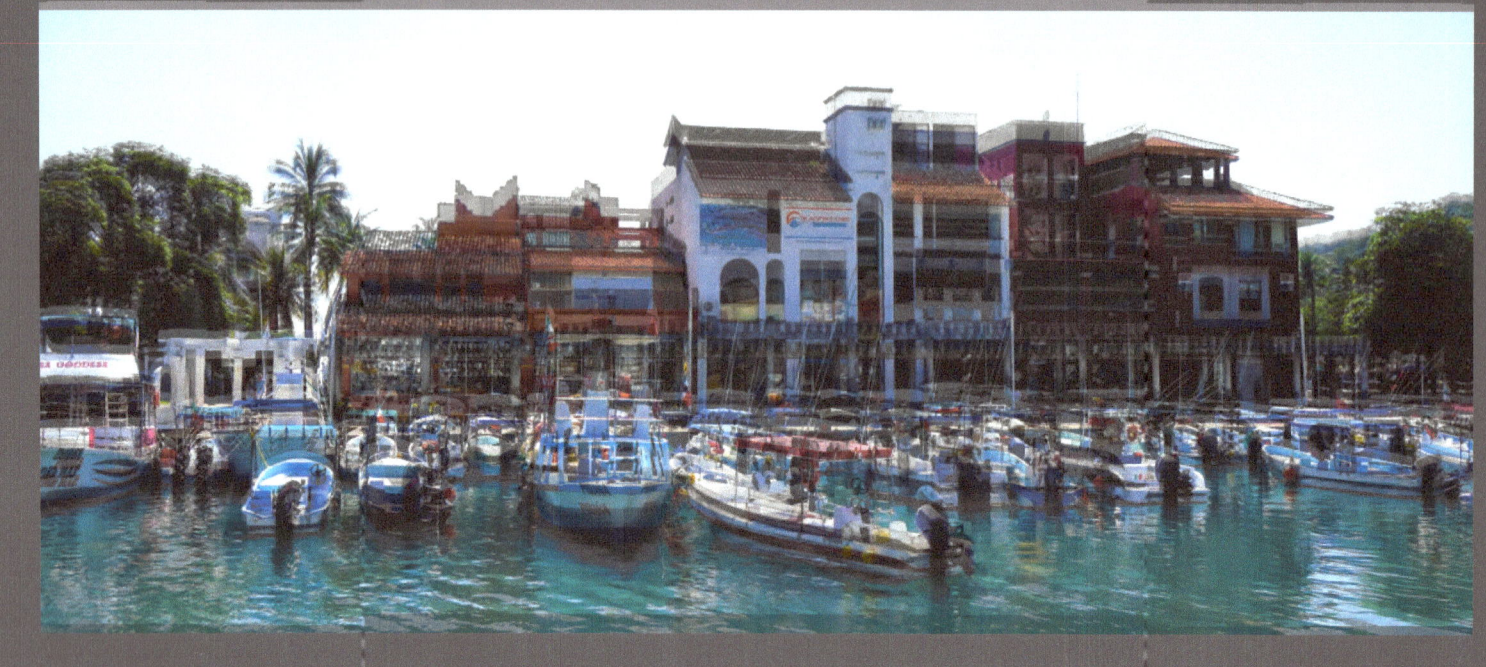

Huatulco Marina

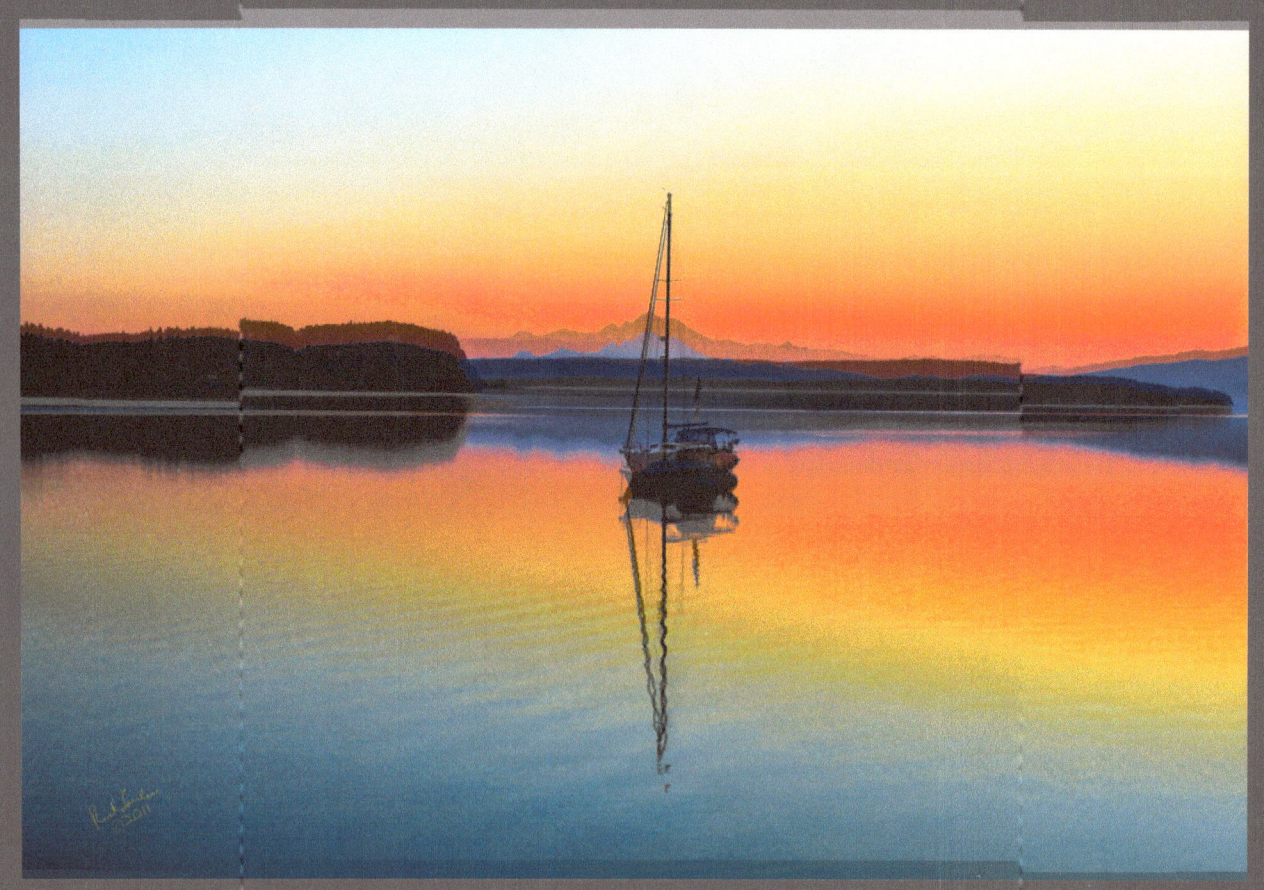

Morning Reflection

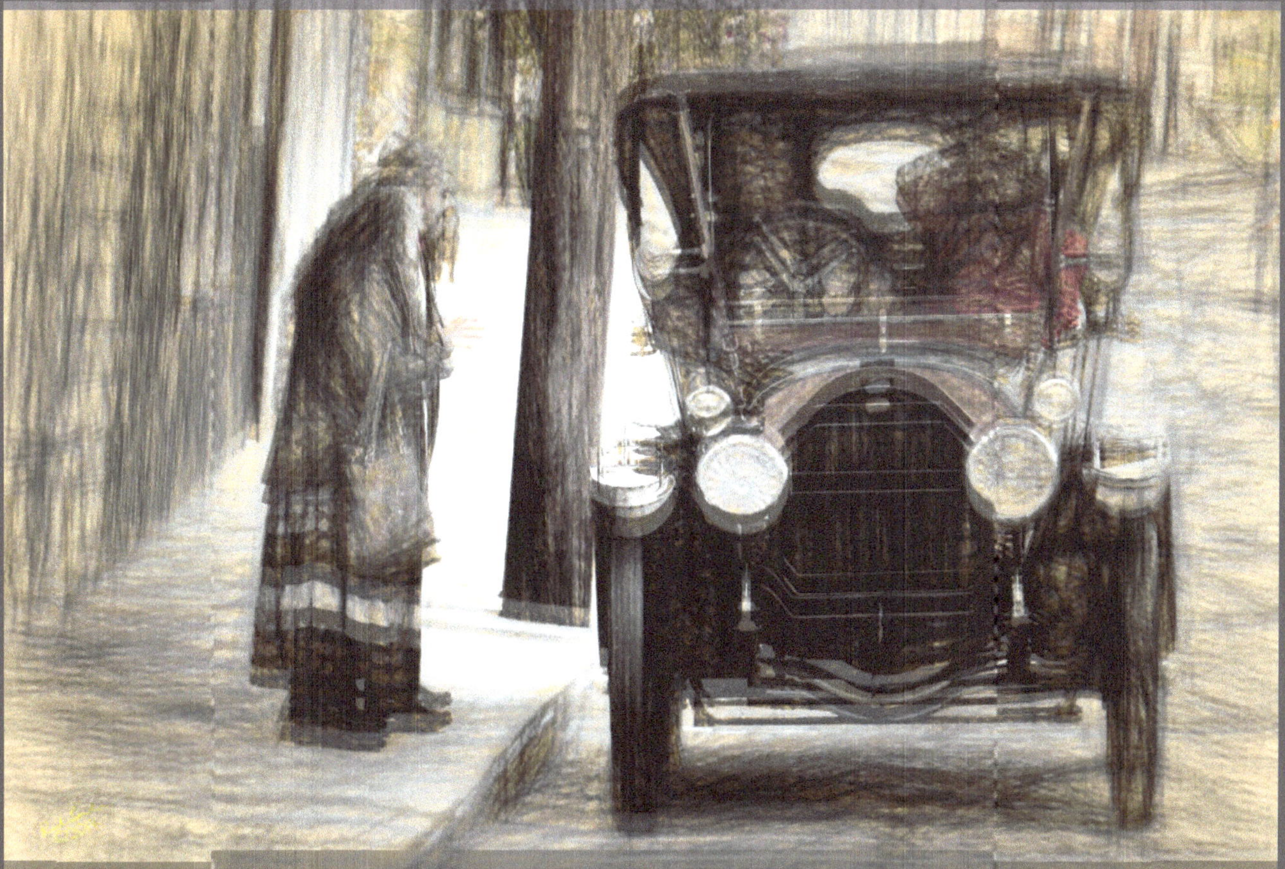

The Conversation

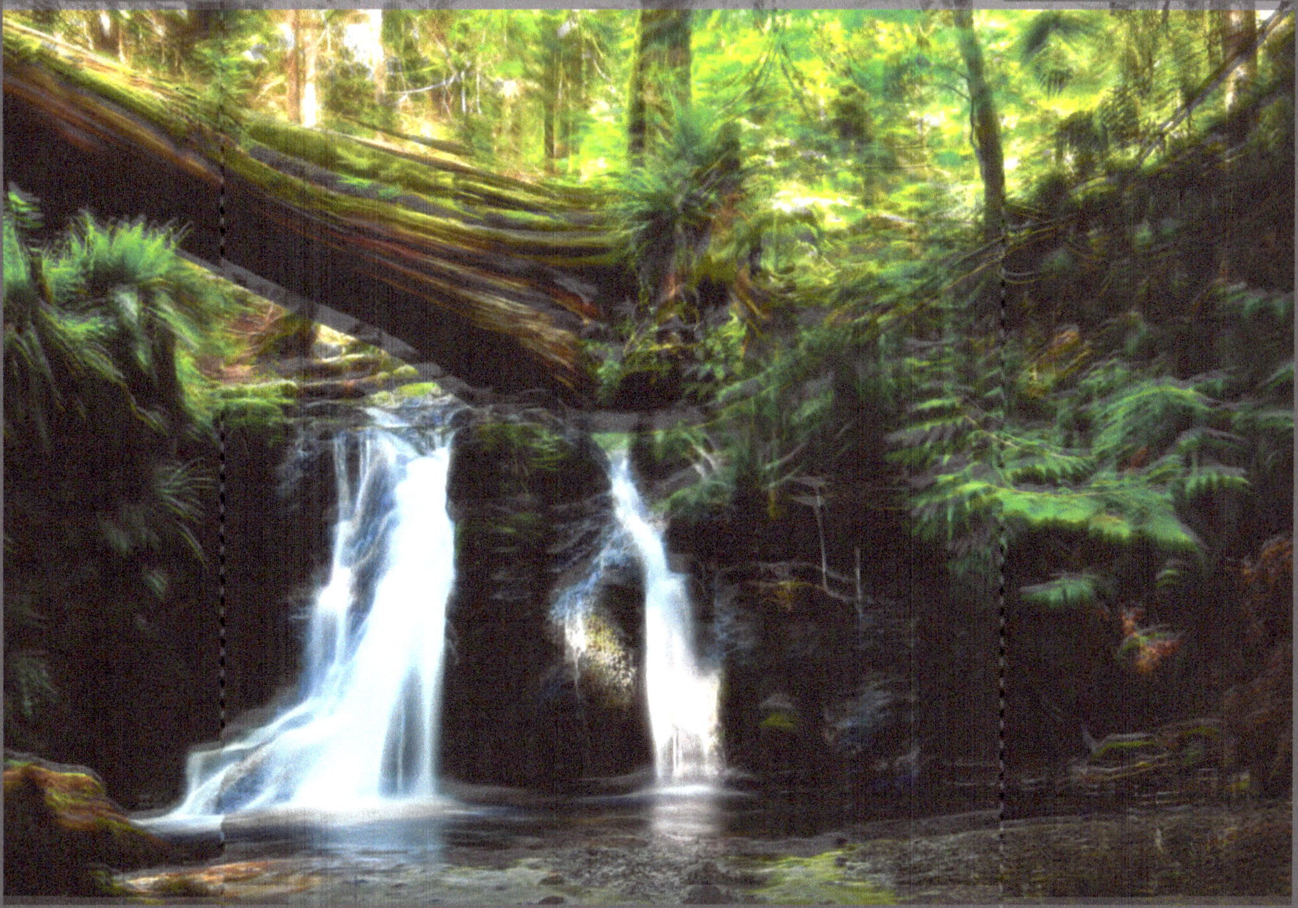

Cascade Falls

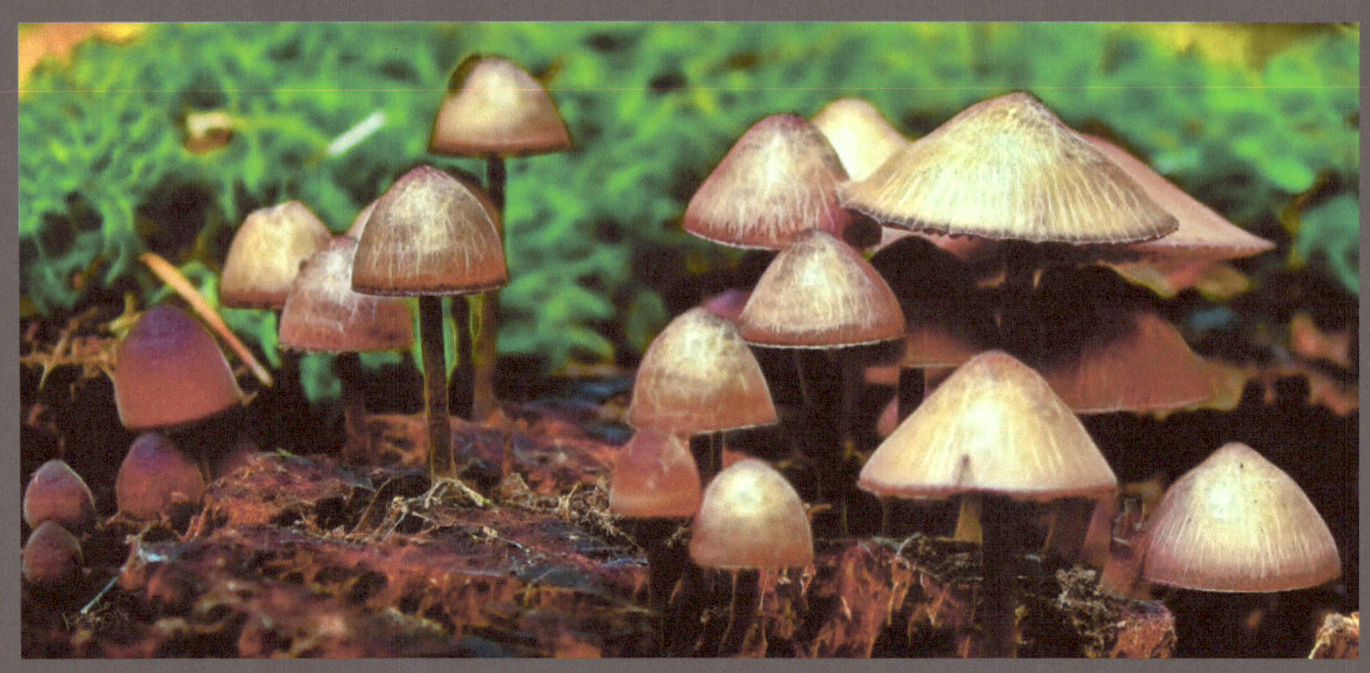

Mushroom Family

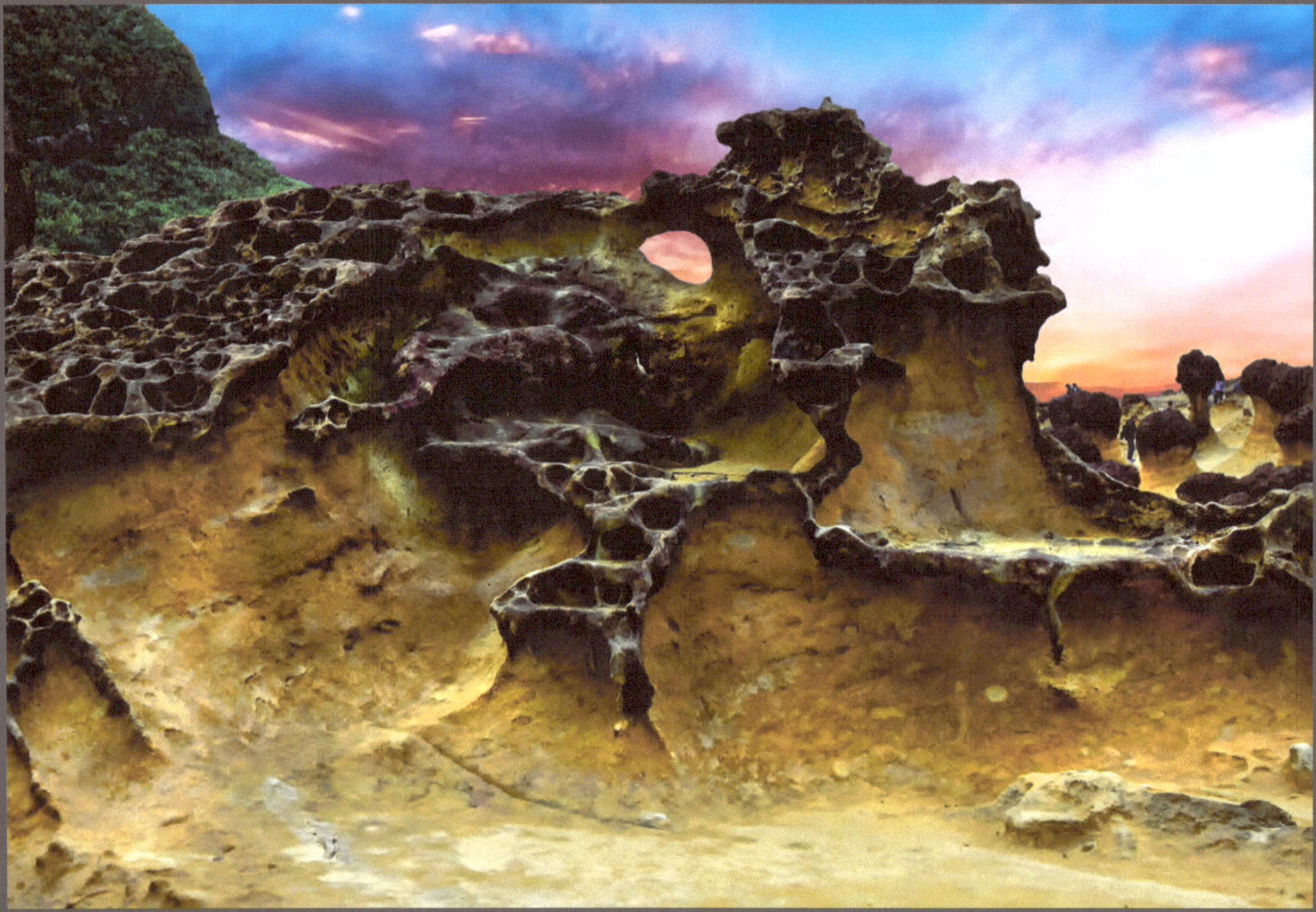

Yehliu Geopark

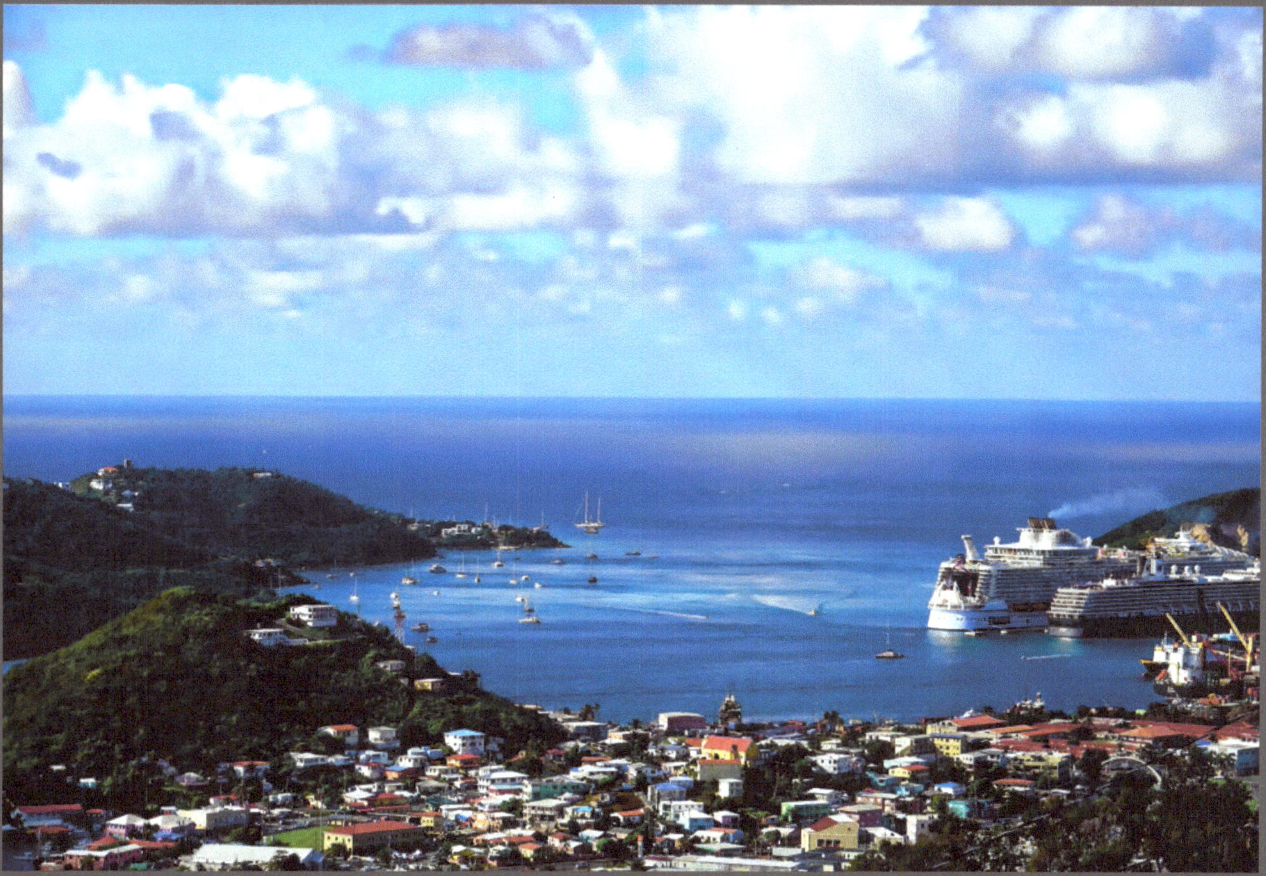

Virgin Island View

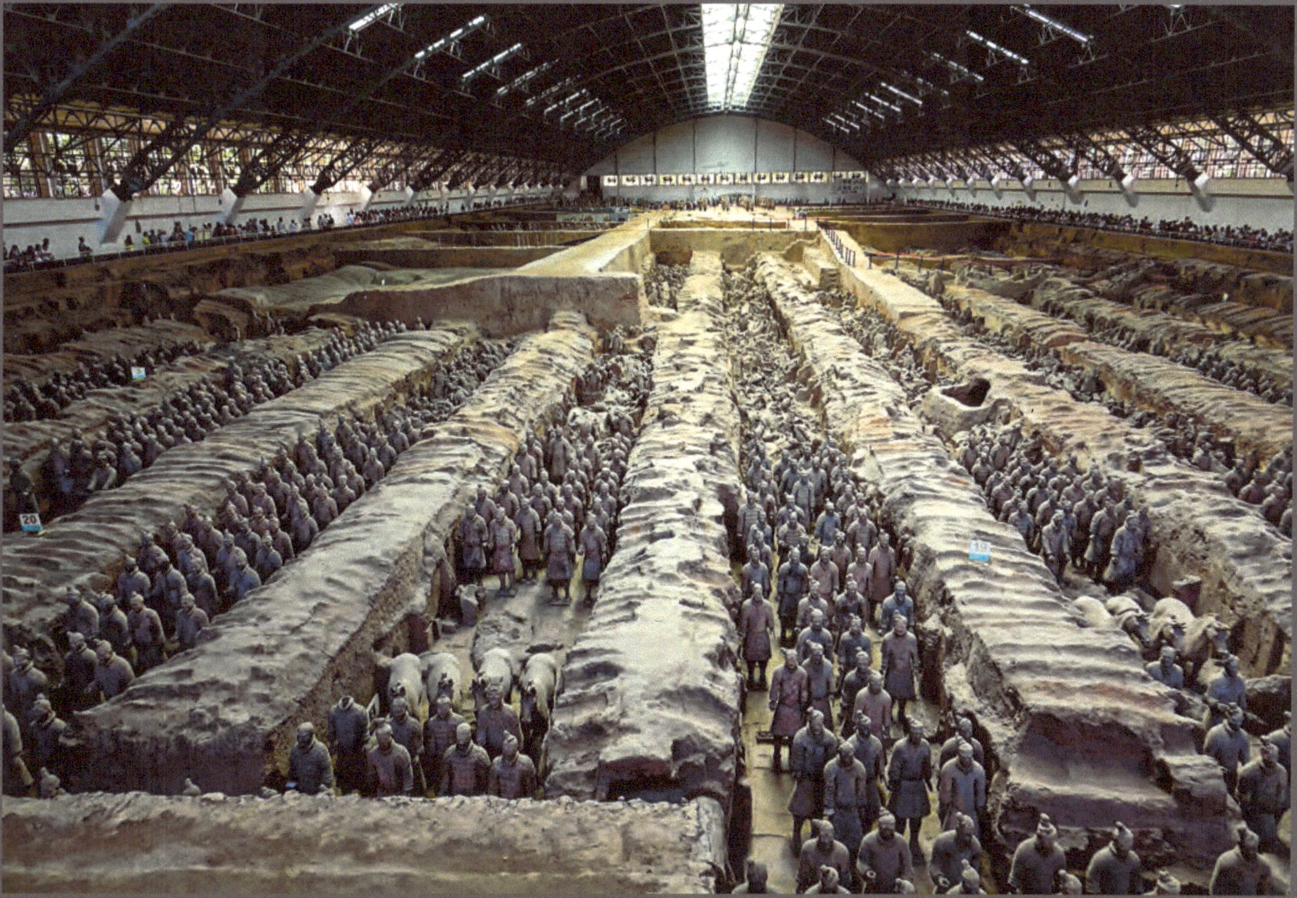

Army Arrayed

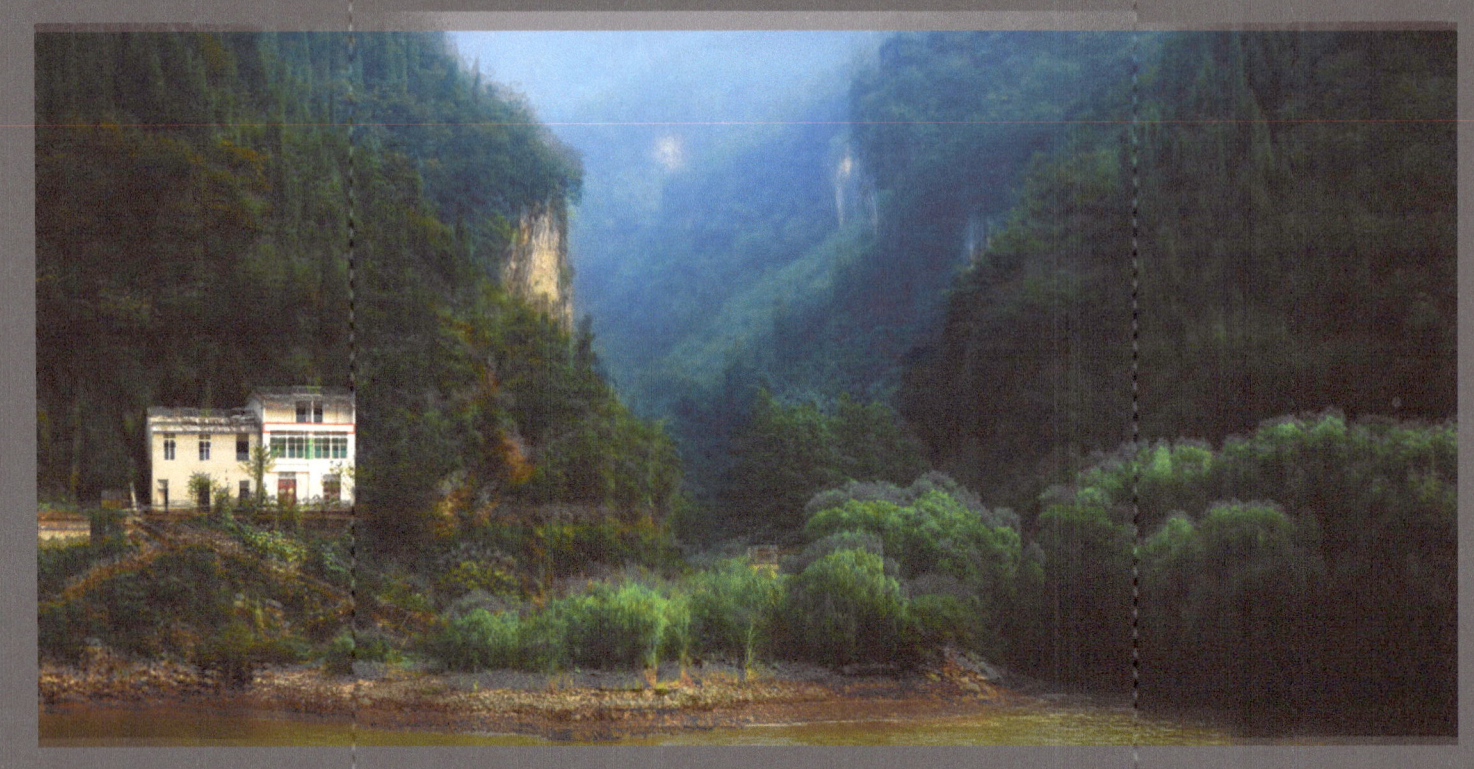
Green Along the Yangtzee

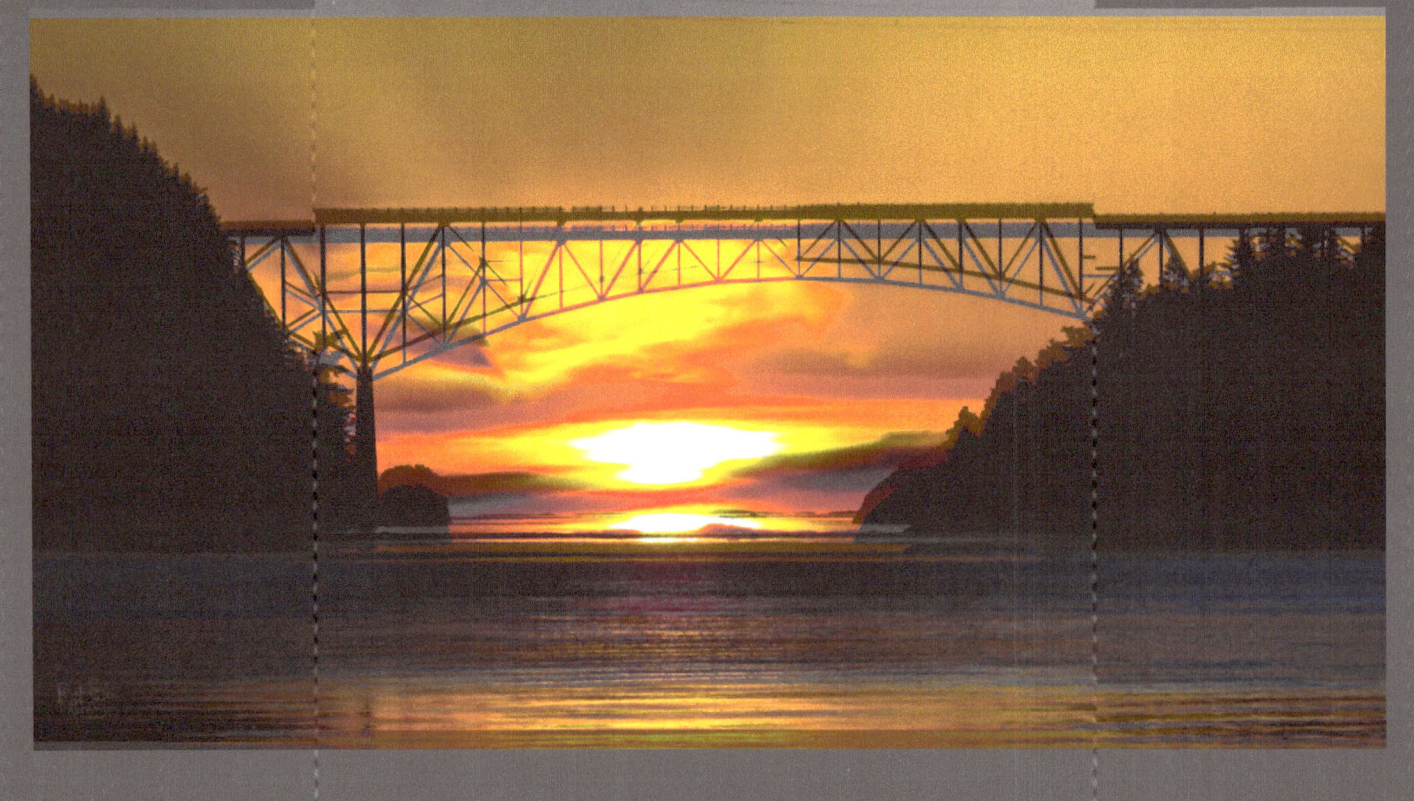
Sunset Bridge

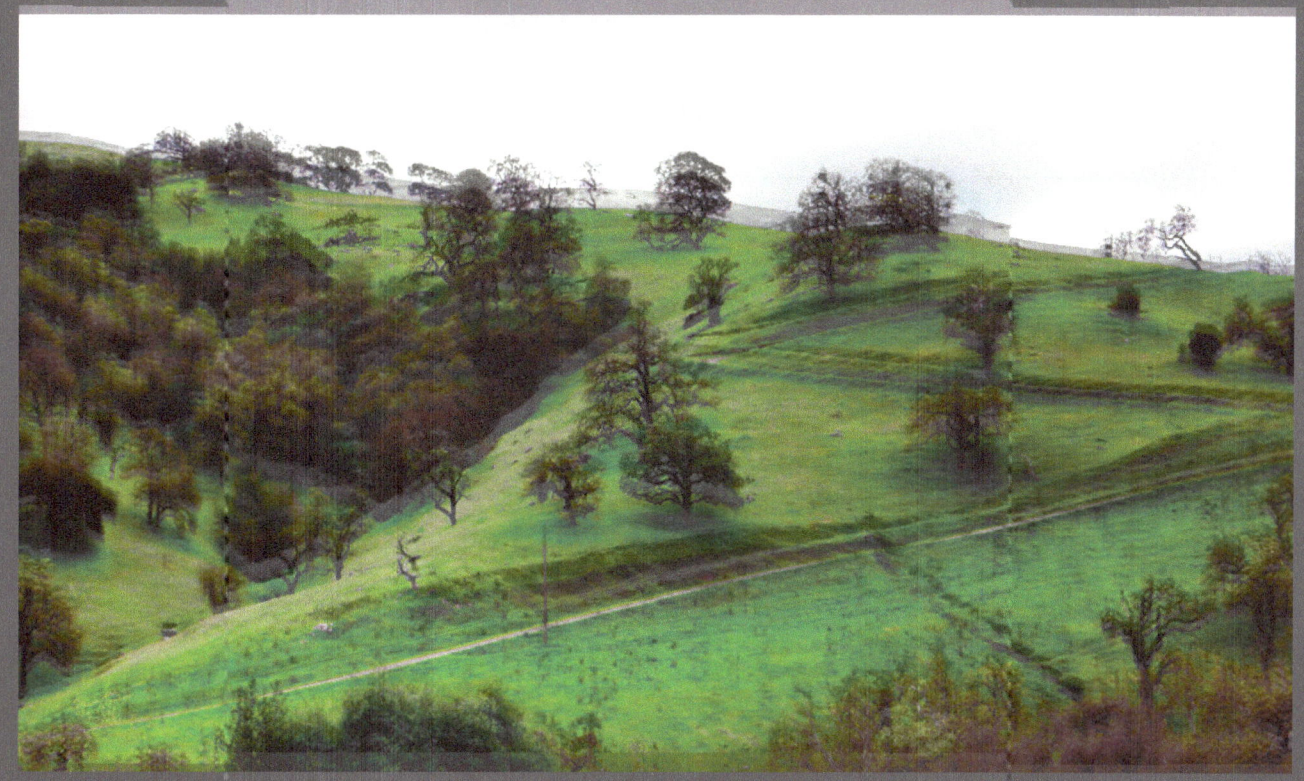
Zorro Country

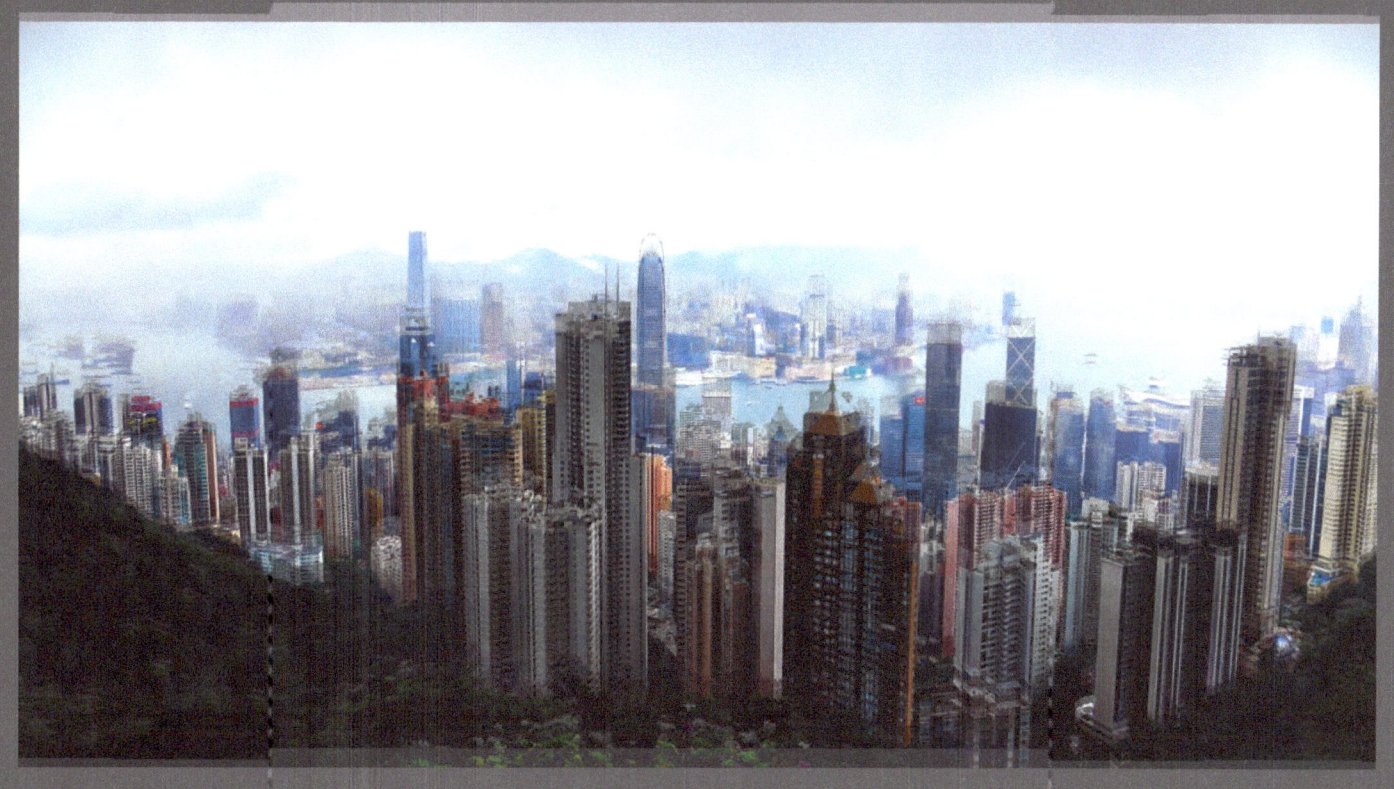
Hong Kong Skyline

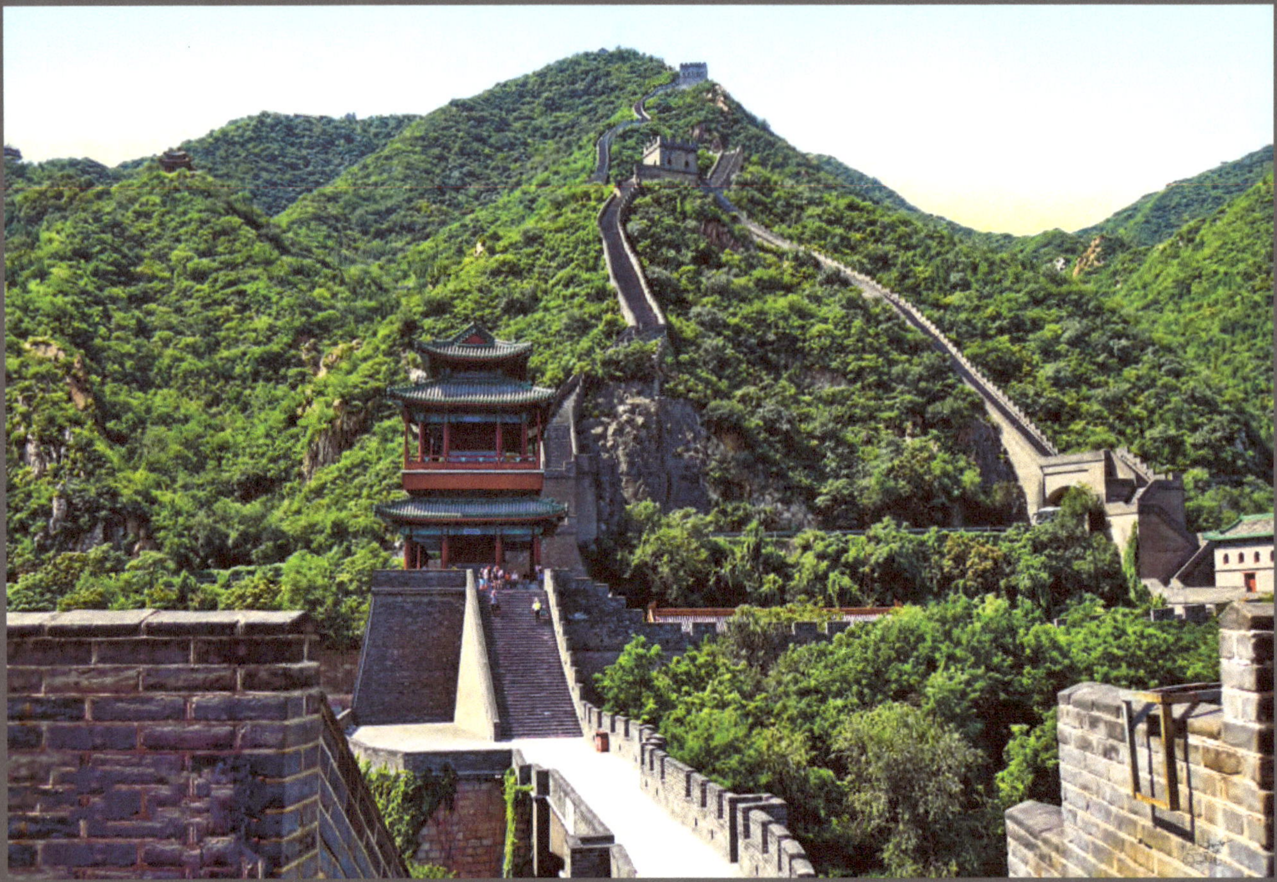

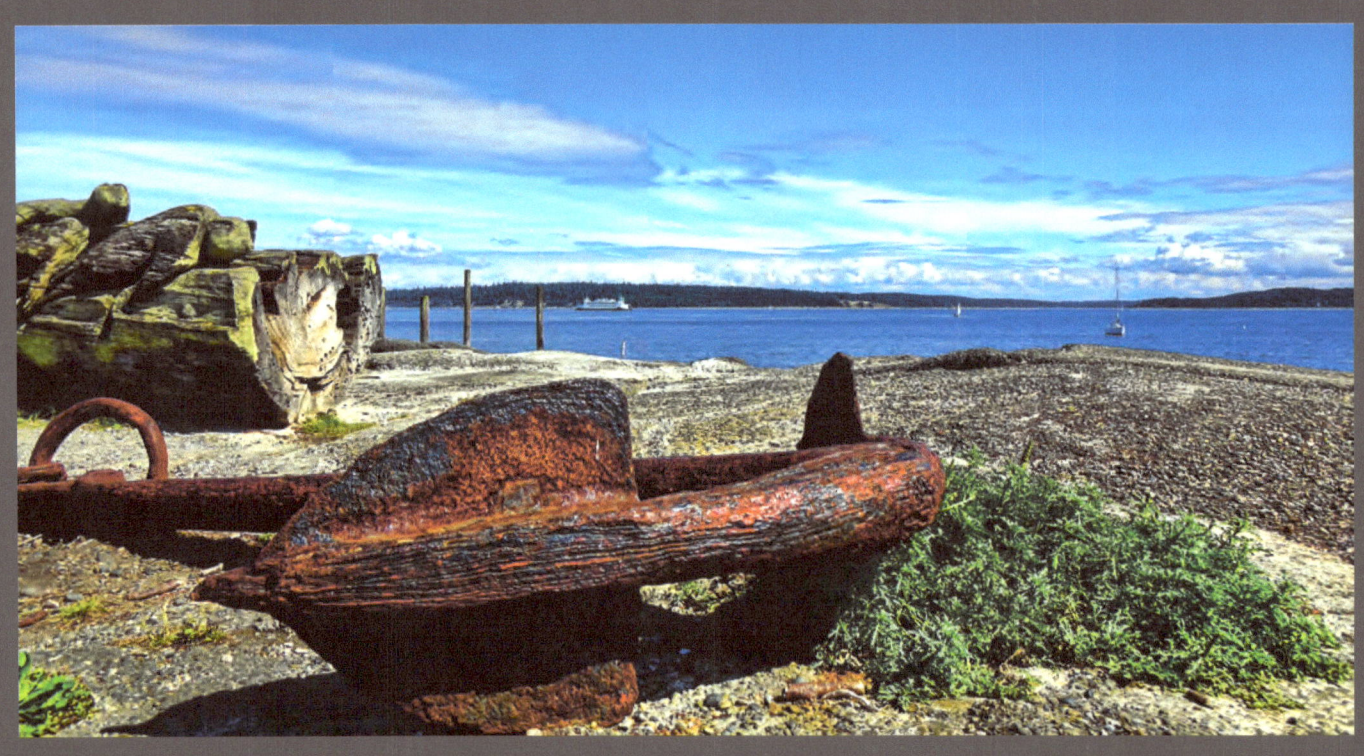

The Wall

Anchors Stay

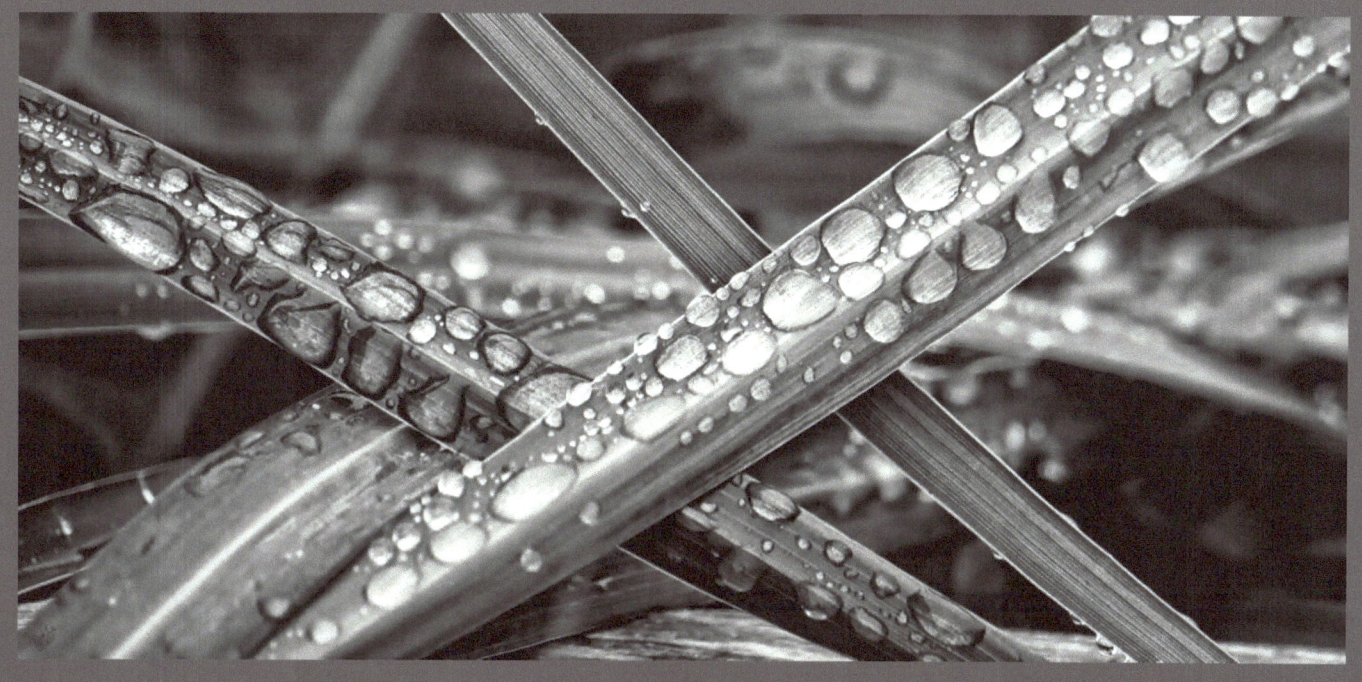

Raindrops on Grass

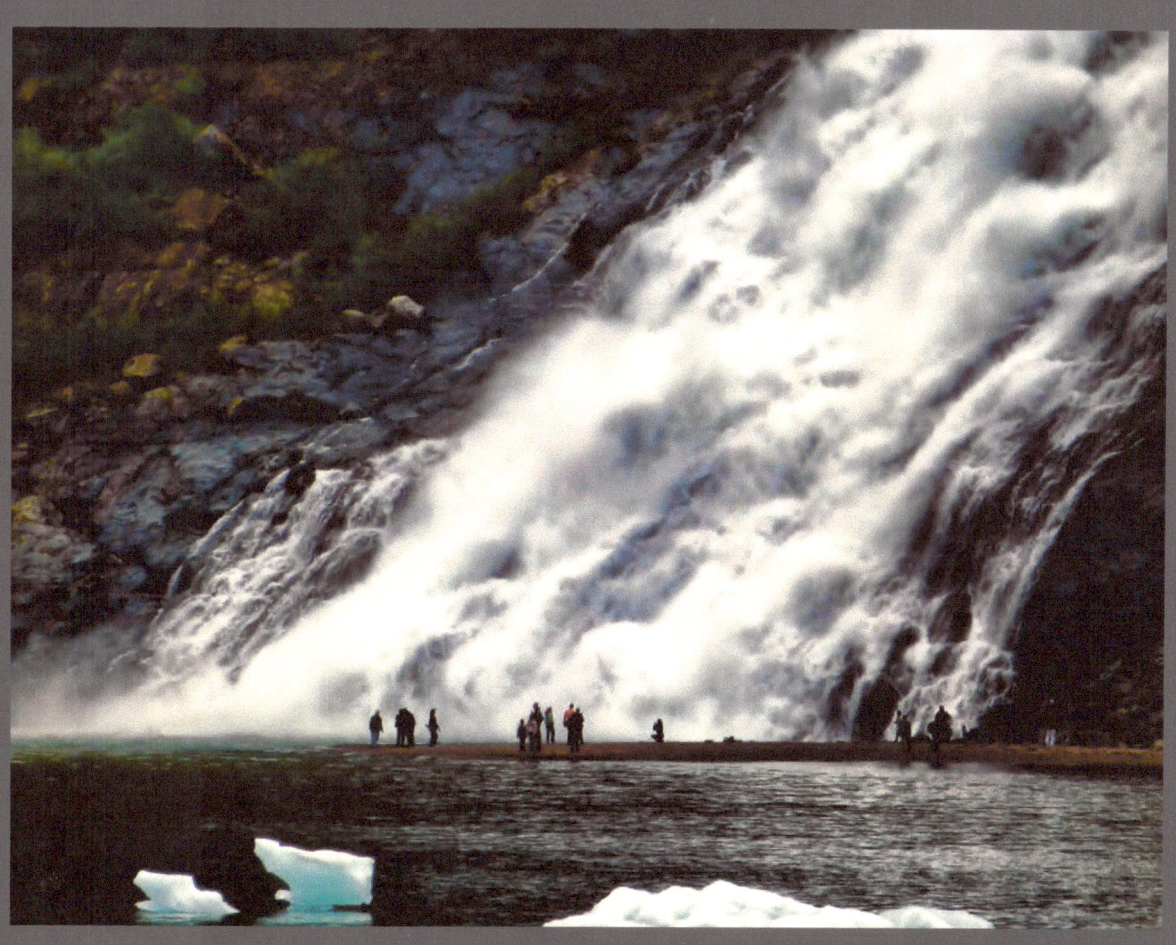

The Falls

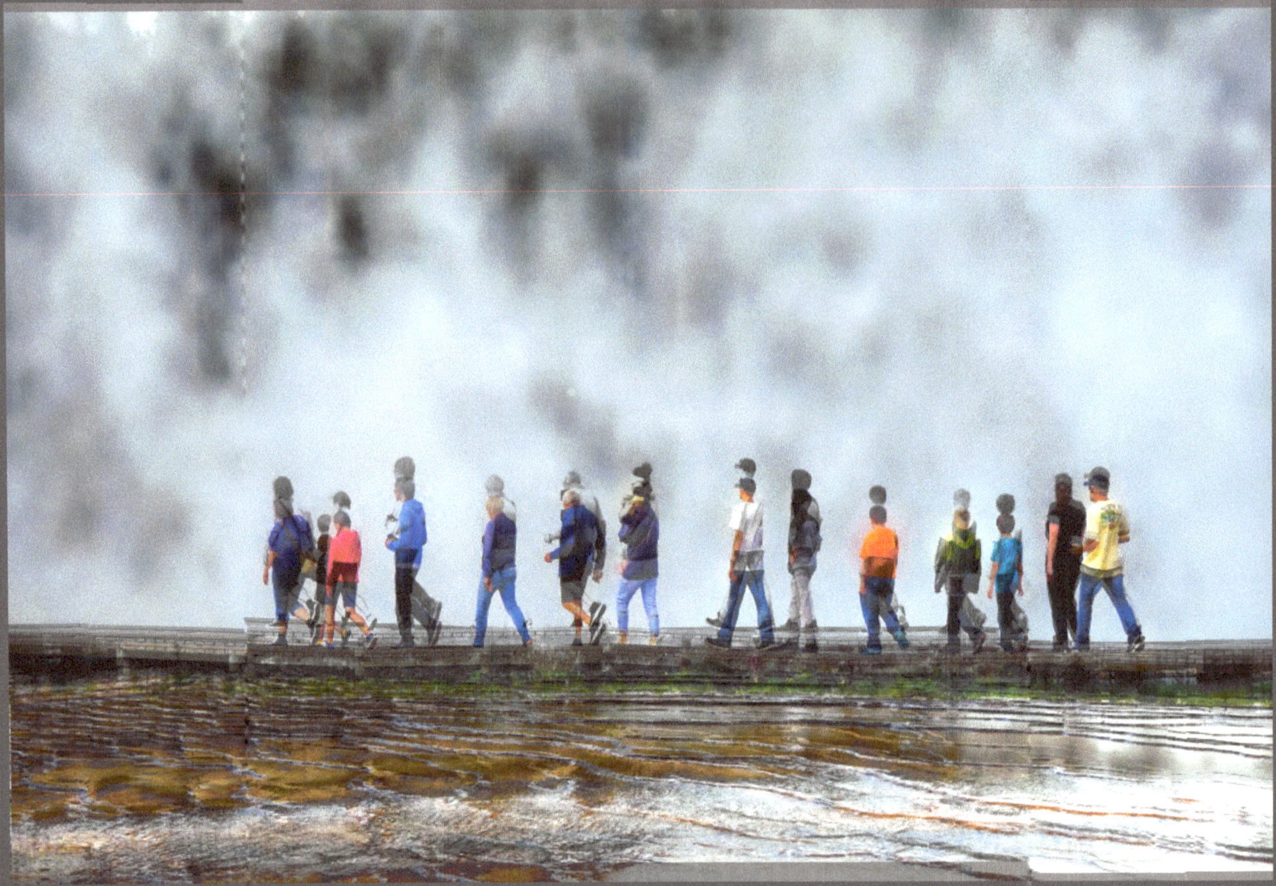

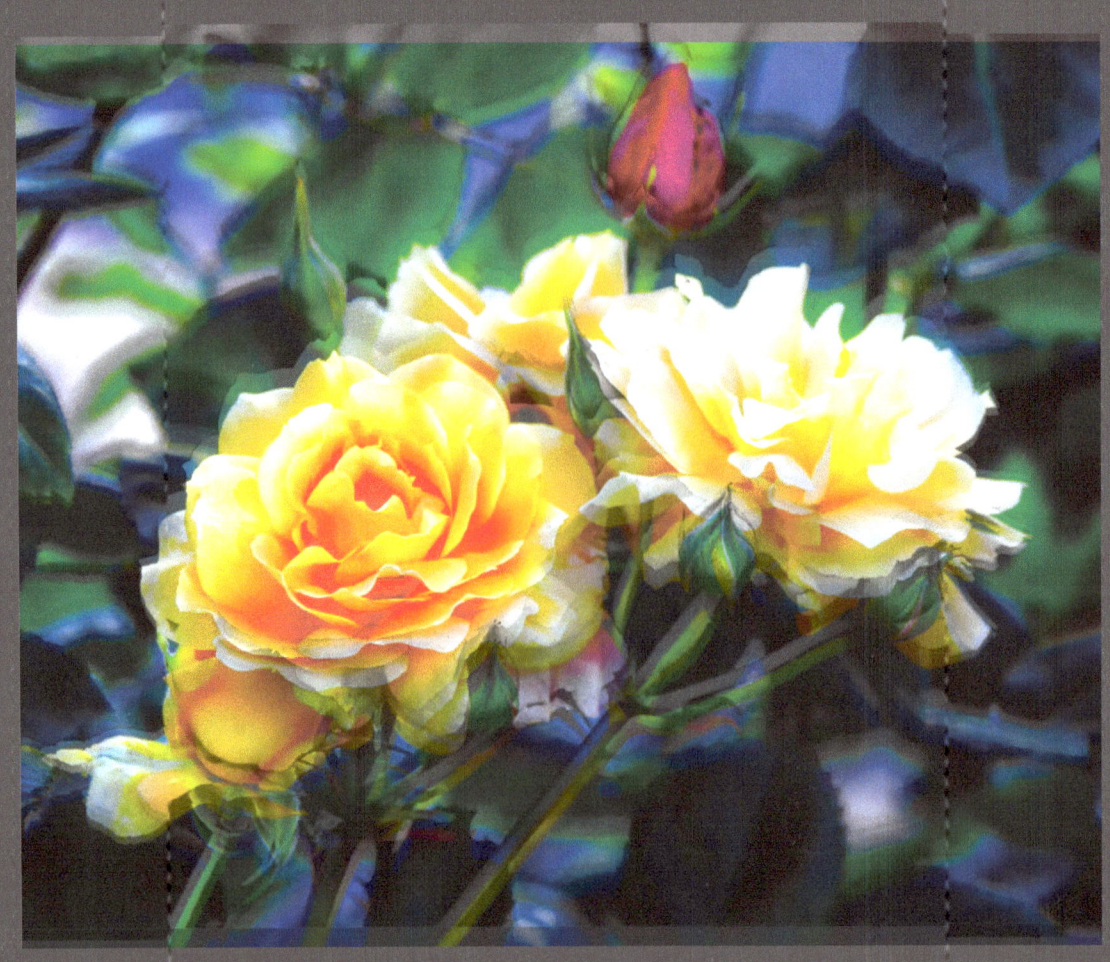

Yellowstone Lineup

Yellow Rose of Portland

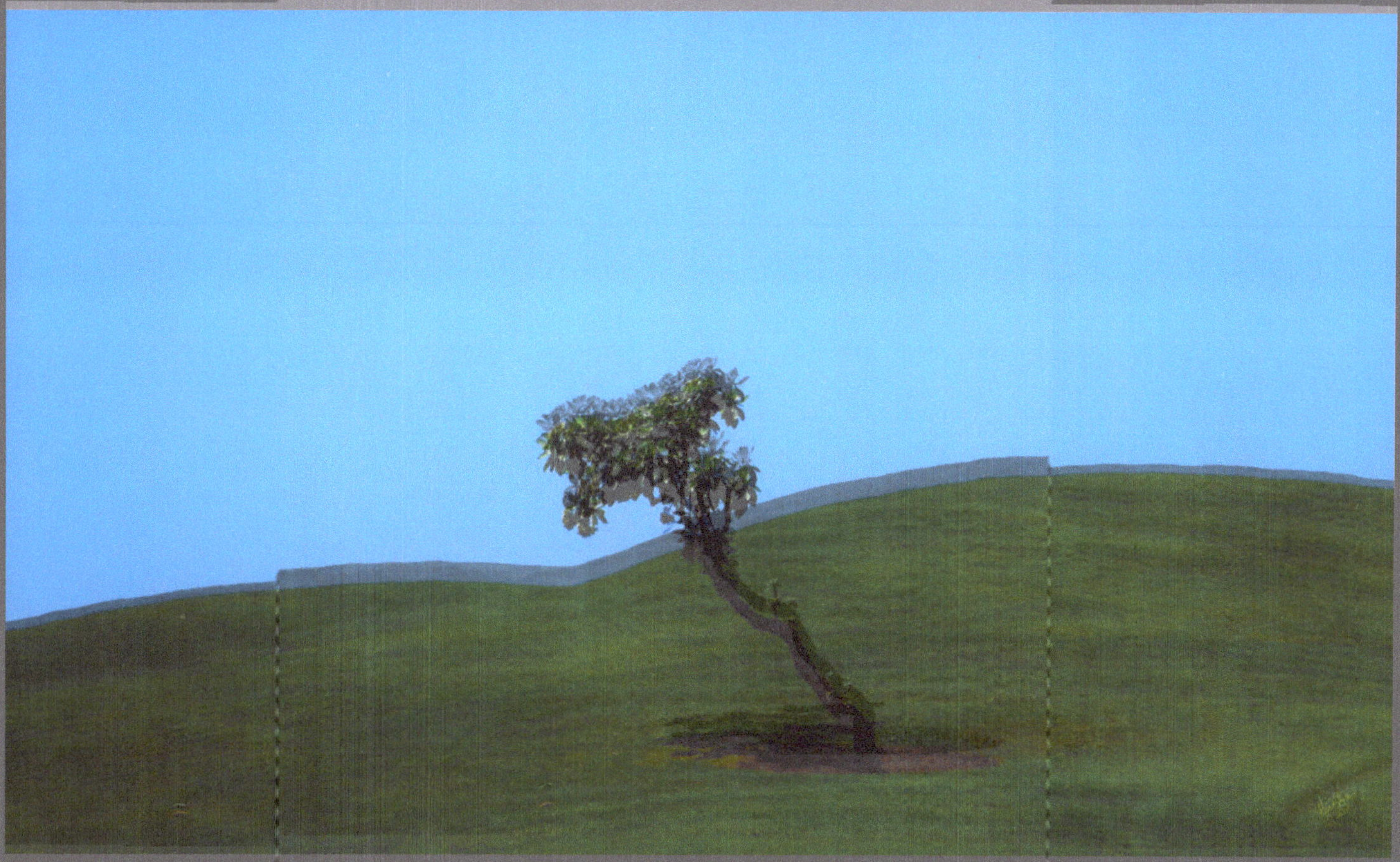

Fairway Tree

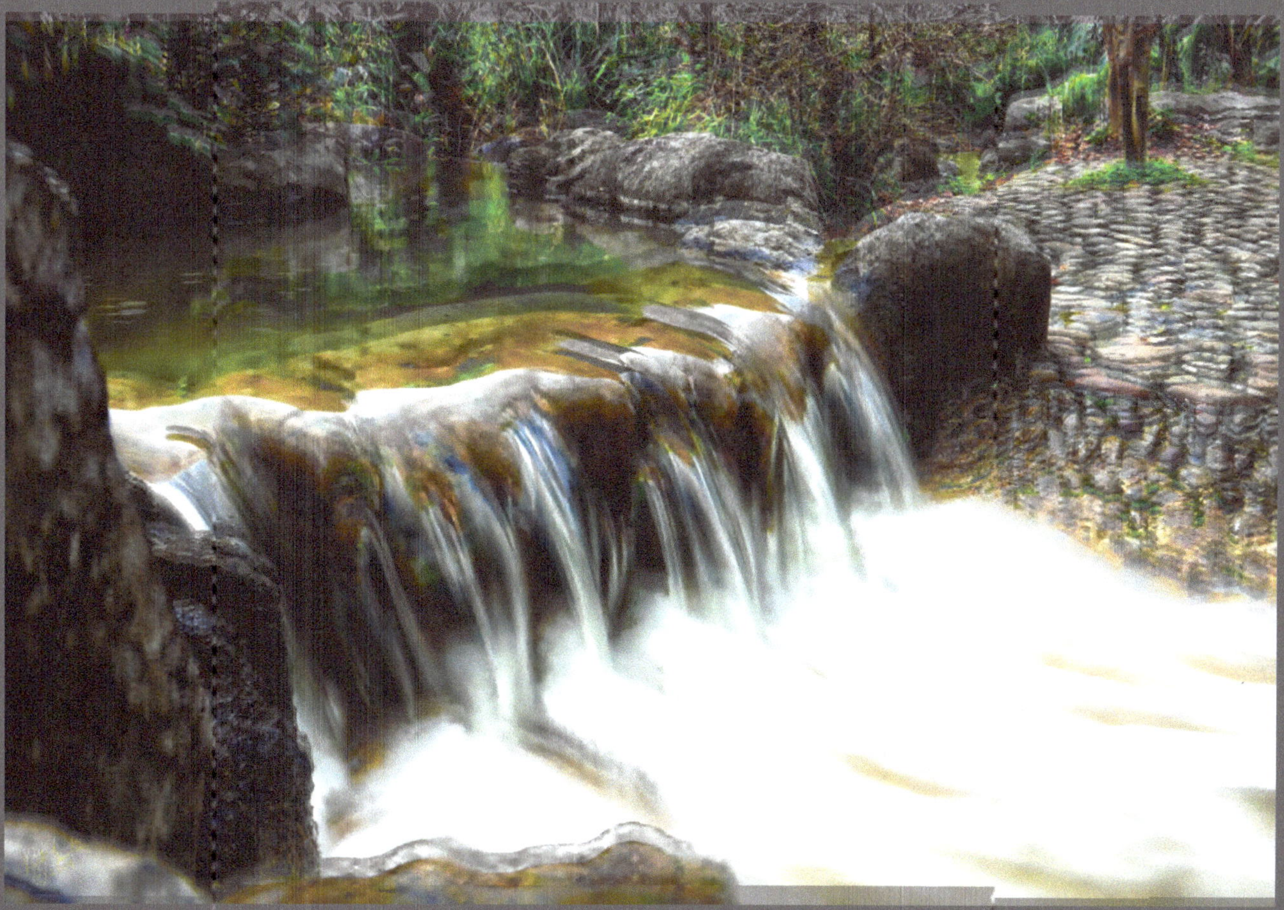

Peaceful Falls

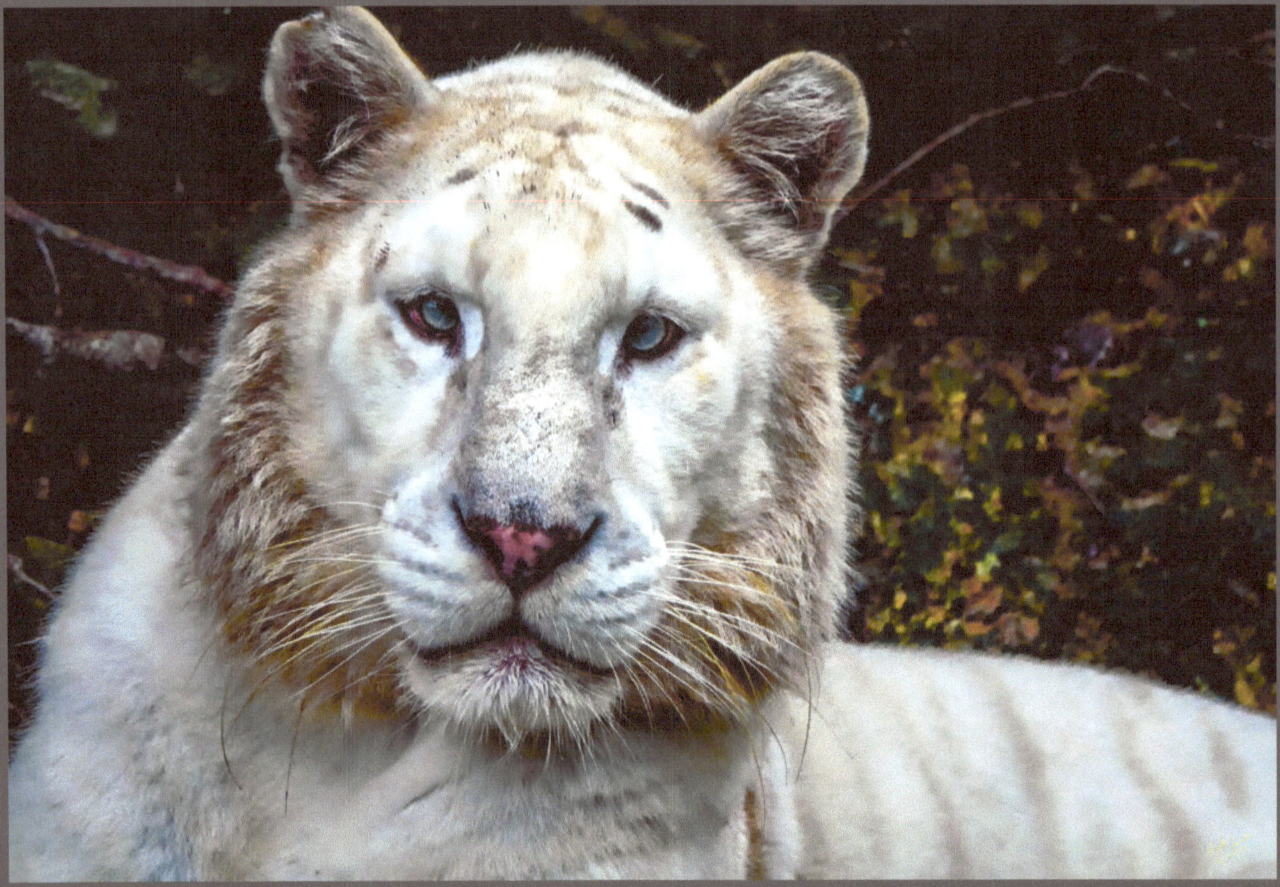

White Tiger

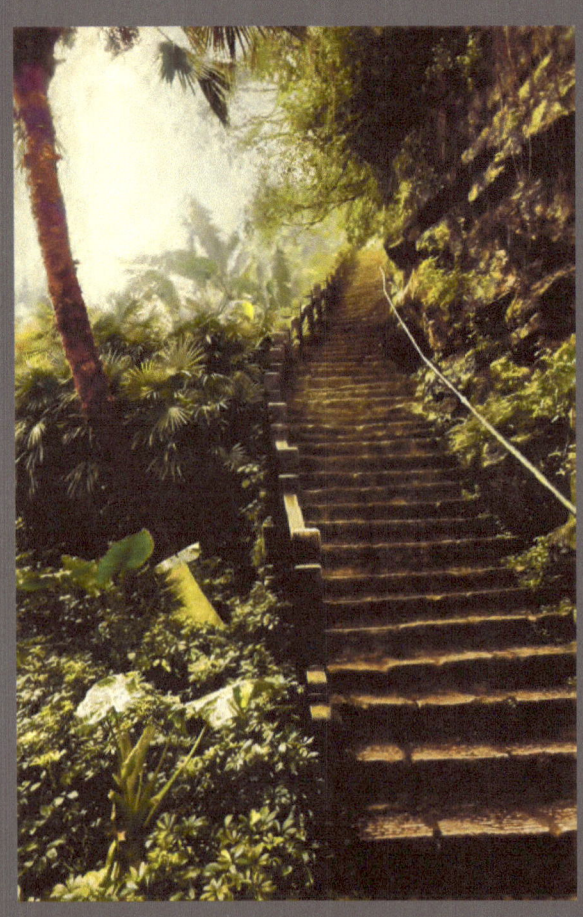

Stairway to Yesterday

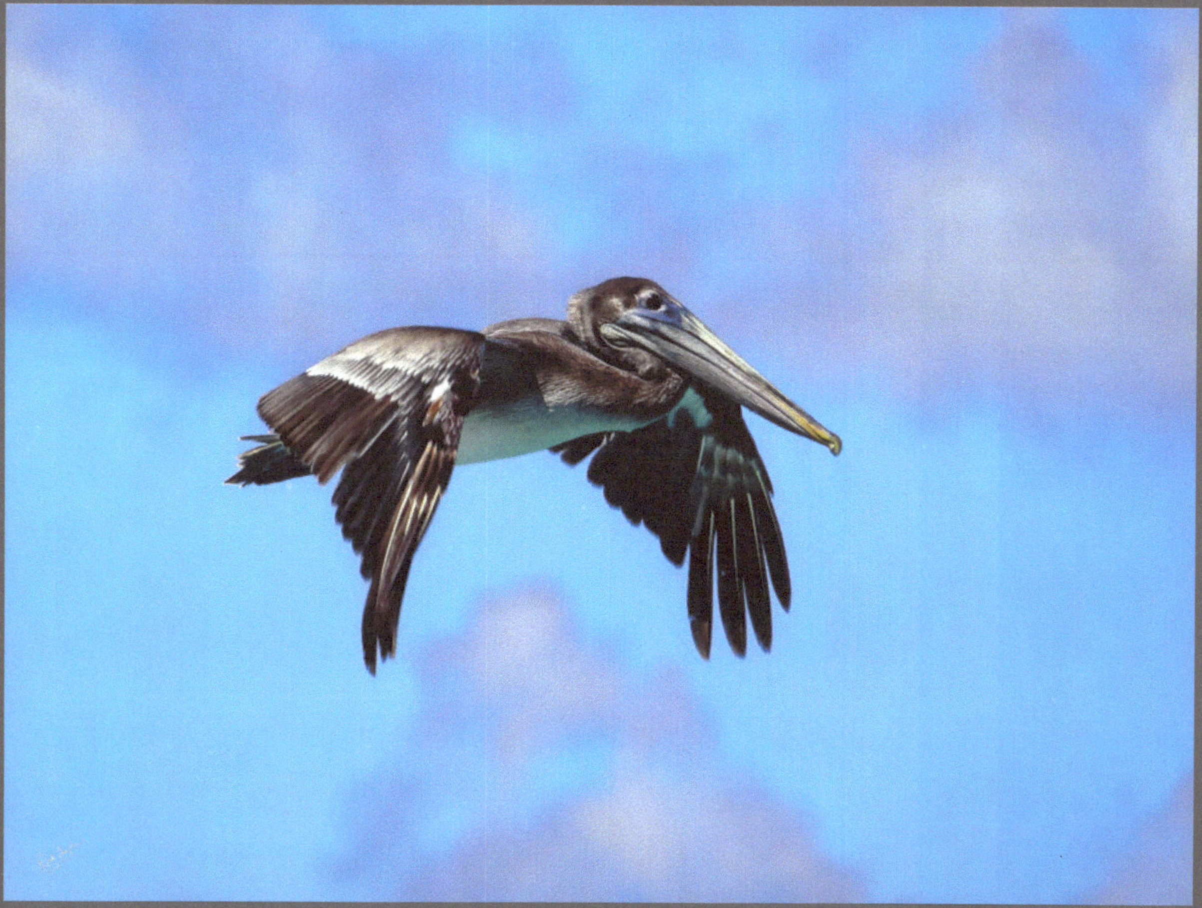

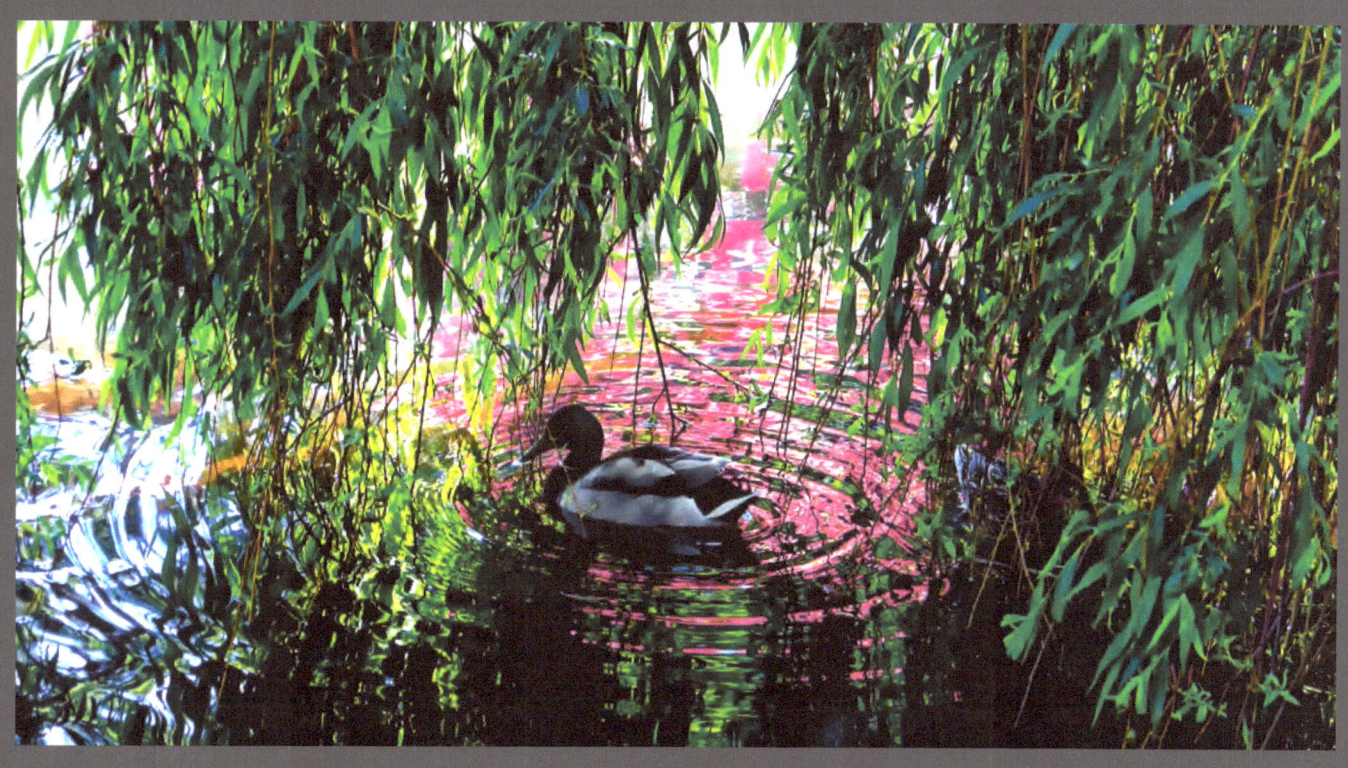

Pelican Flight

Duck in Color

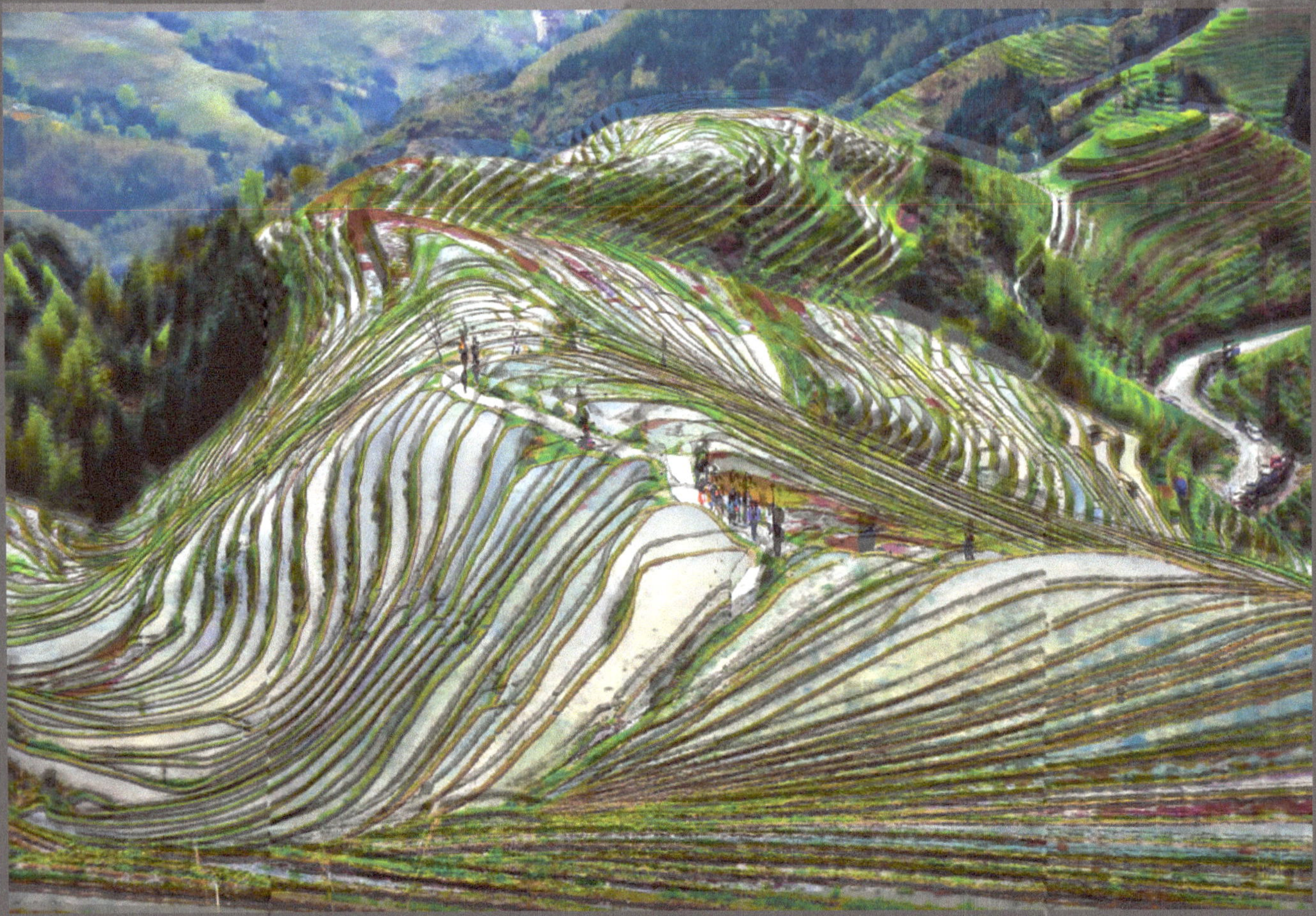

Longji Rice Terraces

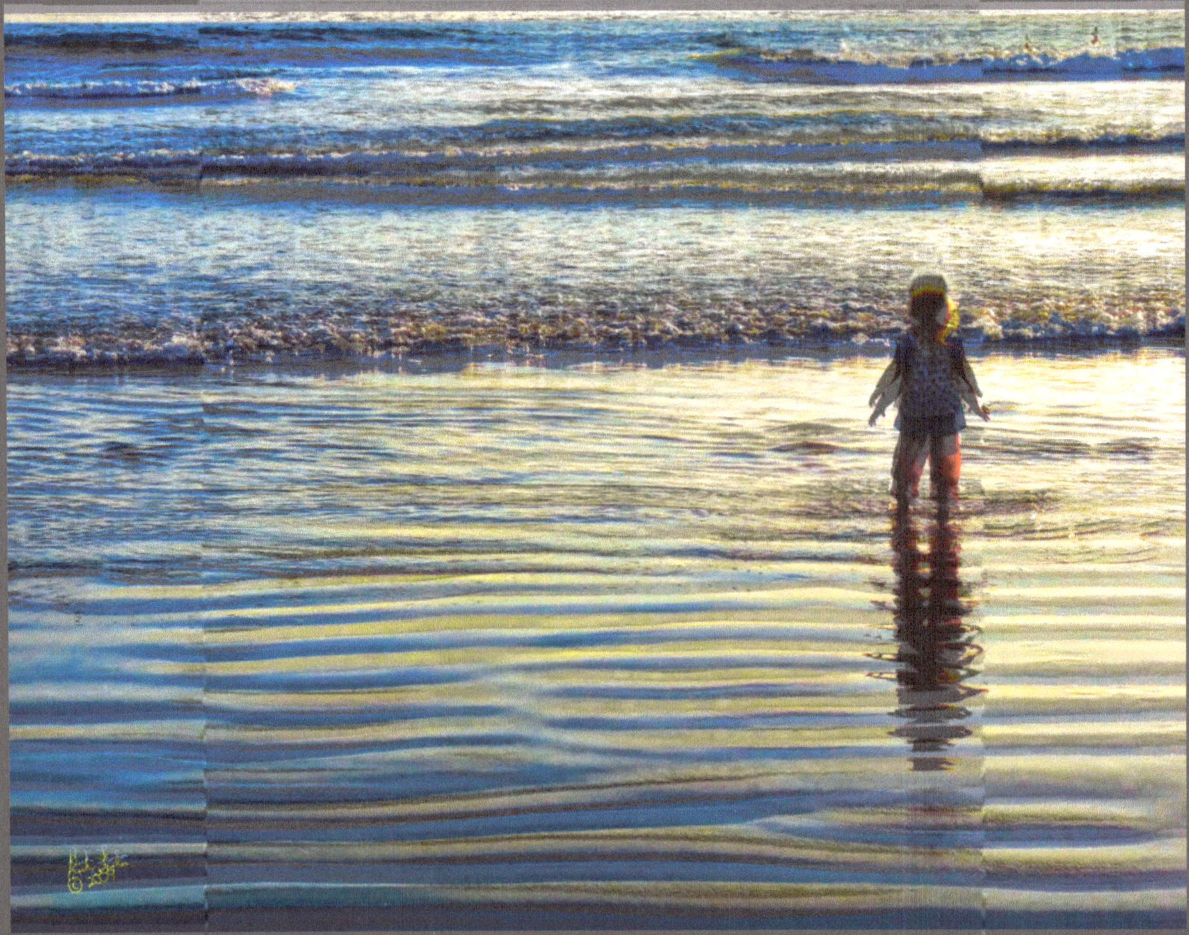

Oceanside Ocean

Eye of the Beholder Photo List

Page 5T: Minding the Sun, Cap Sante Park, Anacortes, Washington
Page 5B: La Push, Washington, Sunset at Beach 1.
Page 6T: Napali Coast Green, Kauai, Hawaii
Page 6B: Riding the Dream, Half Moon Key, Bahamas
Page 7T: Mt. Shuksan Reflection, Picture Lake, Mt. Baker National Forest, Washington
Page 7B: Westlake China, Westlake, Hangzhou, China
Page 8T: Cascade, Sol Duc Falls, Olympic National Park, Washington
Page 8B: Penn Cove Sunrise, Coupeville, Whidbey Island, Washington
Page 9T: Coupeville Classic Cars, Coupeville, Whidbey Island, Washington
Page 9B: Sleeping Giant, Mt. St. Helens, Washington
Page 10T: Magic Landscape, Skagit Valley Tulip Festival, Winter on Mt. Baker, Washington
Page 10B: Lingering Garden, Suzhou, China
Page 11T: Rain Flower, Hong Kong
Page 11B: Resting Place, Space Shuttle Discovery at the Smithsonian Air & Space Museum
Page 12T: Shanghai at Night, Shanghai, China
Page 12B: Wheels of Progress, Snoqualmie, Washington, Railroad Community Park
Page 13T: Ebey's Landing Sunset, Whidbey Island, Washington
Page 13B: L Pod Leap, Near San Juan Island, Washington
Page 14T: Avatar Mountains, Zhangjiajie, China
Page 14B: Wysteria Bee, Compass Rose B&B, Coupeville, Whidbey Island, Washington
Page 15T: Cartagena Old Town, Cartagena, Colombia
Page 15B: Lingshan Grand Buddha, Wuxi, China
Page 16T: The Stare, Point Defiance Zoo, Tacoma, Washington
Page 16B: Flight of the Snow Geese, Skagit Valley, Washington
Page 17T: Stanley Park Reflection, Vancouver, British Columbia
Page 17B: Just A Few Trees, Honolulu Zoo, Oahu, Hawaii
Page 18T: A Bridge, Westlake, Hangzhou, China
Page 18B: Terracotta Warriors Xi'an, China
Page 19T: Snoqualmie Falls, Washington
Page 19B: Spring Arbor, Central Whidbey Island, Washington
Page 20T: Taking Flight, Deception Pass State Park, Whidbey Island, Washington
Page 20B: Raining Sunbeams, Fort Casey State Park, Whidbey Island, Washington
Page 21T: Deception Pass Trail, Deception Pass State Park, Whidbey Island, Washington
Page 21B: Admiralty Head Lighthouse, Fort Casey State Park, Whidbey Island, Washington
Page 22T: The Red Chairs, Lynden, Washington
Page 22B: Juan de Fuca Flotilla, The Strait of Juan de Fuca, Washington
Page 23T: School for Mutants, Hatley Park Castle, Colwood, British Columbia
Page 23B: Memorial, Lincoln Memorial, Washington, D.C.
Page 24T: Rainbow Falls, Hilo, Hawaii
Page 24B: Lime Kiln Lighthouse, Lime Kiln State Park, San Juan Island, Washington
Page 25T: D.C. Rendezvous, Tidal Basin, Washington, D.C.
Page 25B: Suva Sailing, Penn Cove, Whidbey Island, Washington
Page 26T: Mt. Constitution, Orcas Island, Washington
Page 26B: The Window, Skagit Valley, Washington
Page 27T: Raindrops on Petals, Oak Harbor, Whidbey Island, Washington
Page 27B: Dancing the Daffodils, Skagit Valley, Washington
Page 28T: Tulip Field, Skagit Valley, Washington
Page 28B: Fog on the Prairie, Ebey's Landing National Historical Reserve, Whidbey Island

Eye of the Beholder Photo List

Page 29T: Calm on the Marina. Oak Harbor Marina, Whidbey Island, Washington
Page 29B: Fog in the Morning. Oak Harbor Marina, Whidbey Island, Washington
Page 30T: Cormorant Pose. Oak Harbor Marina, Whidbey Island, Washington
Page 30B: Season of Leaves. Coupeville, Whidbey Island, Washington
Page 31T: Flowers of My Mind. Coupeville, Whidbey Island, Washington
Page 31B: Gazebo Sunset. Oak Harbor, Whidbey Island, Washington
Page 32T: Battle for Penn Cove. Coupeville, Whidbey Island, Washington
Page 32B: The Eagle Has Landed. West Beach, Oak Harbor, Whidbey Island, Washington
Page 33T: Preparing for the Race. Penn Cove, Coupeville, Whidbey Island, Washington
Page 33B: Beach Rocks. Deception Pass State Park, Whidbey Island, Washington
Page 34T: Huatulco Marina. Huatulco, Mexico
Page 34B: Morning Reflection. Penn Cove, Coupeville, Whidbey Island, Washington
Page 35T: The Conversation. Coupeville, Whidbey Island, Washington
Page 35B: Cascade Falls. Upper Cascade Falls, Orcas Island, Washington
Page 36T: Mushroom Family. Whidbey Island, Washington
Page 36B: Yehliu Geopark. Taiwan
Page 37T: Virgin Island View. St. Thomas, U.S. Virgin Islands
Page 37B: Army Arrayed. Xi'an, China
Page 38T: Green Along the Yangtzee. Yangtzee River, China
Page 38B: Sunset Bridge. Deception Pass Bridge, Whidbey Island, Washington
Page 39T: Zorro Country. Along Highway 152 near Casa de Fruta, Central California
Page 39B: Hong Kong Skyline. Victoria Peak, Hong Kong
Page 40T: The Wall. Great Wall of China near Beijing, China
Page 40B: Anchors Stay. Port Townsend, Washington
Page 41T: Raindrops on Grass. Ala Spit, Whidbey Island, Washington
Page 41B: The Falls. Nugget Falls, Mendenhall Glacier, Juneau, Alaska
Page 42T: Yellowstone Lineup. Yellowstone National Park, Montana
Page 42B: Yellow Rose of Portland. Rose Garden, Portland, Oregon
Page 43T: Fairway Tree. Kauai, Hawaii
Page 43B: Peaceful Falls. Seven Star Park, Guilin, China
Page 44T: White Tiger. Chimelong Safari Park, Guangzhou, China
Page 44B: Stairway to Yesterday. Elephant Trunk Hill, Guilin, China
Page 45T: Pelican Flight. St. Thomas, U.S. Virgin Islands
Page 45B: Duck in Color. Beacon Hill Park, Victoria, B.C.
Page 46T: Lonji Rice Terraces. Longsheng, China.
Page 46B: Oceanside Ocean. Oceanside, California

www.ingramcontent.com/pod-product-compliance
Lightning Source LLC
Chambersburg PA
CBHW051951210526
45473CB00019B/1147